M. Y. GINZBURG

RHYTHM
IN ARCHITECTURE

Artifice
books on architecture

*Dedicated to the bright
memory of my late friend N.A.K.*

PART ONE

ANALYSIS OF RHYTHM

FOREWORD

Among the arts, architecture occupies a rather special place. On the one hand, it is the result of a multiplicity of utilitarian, material, and structural conditions; on the other, it is a world of forms which are of value in themselves and which are abstract to an extreme extent. Whereas in their abstract manifestations the other plastic arts are nevertheless subject to some degree of depictiveness, a certain amount of non-formal content, architecture, like music, is in this respect the purest of all the arts.

From the moment when it came into existence until the present time, in its formal elements, particular articulations, and composition of masses, architecture has been inspired only by the laws of rhythm; these laws determine the true essence of all works of architecture. The entire history of architecture is essentially the history of various manifestations of these extremely pure dynamic laws.

In the Parthenon and the Palazzo Pitti, the Cathedral at Reims, and the Dormition Cathedral in Vladimir, and all other monuments which differ in terms of their formal qualities, we see the eternally effective principle of rhythm.

The present book is an attempt to bring to light this true essence of architecture. It is merely an experiment, and as such should be regarded with indulgence.

Moscow, January 1922

I.

The universe is permeated with rhythm. We encounter its laws in the movement of the planetary systems, in man as he works, in the flexing of the wild animal, and in the flowing stream of the river. It matters not to what science we turn or on what vital process we dwell: everywhere we shall see a manifestation of rhythm.

All scientific hypotheses, laws, and philosophical viewpoints are nothing other than an attempt to find formulae and definitions that express the rhythmic beating of the cosmos.

Likewise, man's internal world—the activities of his lungs and heart, the movement of his hands and feet—is subject to the laws of rhythm, which are an element of psycho-physical nature.

Numerous travellers and historians of culture have observed that in negroes, Arabs, and Zulus all their movements, dances, songs, games, and work preserve a constant sense of rhythm—a sense which they maintain with great precision since it derives from man's organic essence.

Rhythm is a kind of supreme regulator, a wise helmsman directing all manifestations of activity throughout the universe.

It serves not just to make our work easier, but also as a source of aesthetic pleasure, an element of art which has been innate in all mankind from savages to the most refined representatives of the most cultured epochs.

It enjoins us to strive for the greatest fullness of pleasure in life while spending as little energy and *joie de vivre* as possible.

The influence of rhythm is something that was noticed by learned people and philosophers in ancient times, and is repeatedly mentioned by Plato and Aristotle. Aristotle notes three kinds of rhythm: rhythm of images (the movements of dance), rhythm of tones (song), and rhythm of speech (metre).*

II.

Art is merely one of the fields in which a sense of rhythm holds sway and plays a guiding role. When materialised through art, rhythm is an essential companion of all the arts.

The essence of every rhythmic manifestation is, above all, *movement.* (The word "rhythm" is Greek for "flow".)

The dynamics of rhythm are determined by a certain alternation of elements and the way in which they move forwards.

One element is replaced by another, and the relation between our perception at a given moment and the perception which we had at the preceding moment is the essence of the feeling of rhythm.

---

*) Karl Bücher, *Work and Rhythm*

Such, for example, is the nature of musical rhythm. A particular sequence of sounds and their constant progressive movement produce a rhythmic impression of song. At each given moment it is not this or that particular sound which is characteristic of the rhythm, but the relation between the nth sound and the n-1th, i.e. the preceding, sound: the relation between the element which exists at the present moment and the preceding element, which remains only in our minds.

This relation of an element which actually exists to one which has been interrupted and is finished in time but still exists thanks to our tendency to remember our perceptions, a relation which creates a certain continuity of impression, is an essential part of music, song, and dance.

An element that is highly characteristic of this kind of rhythm is a particular movement of elements and the way in which they proceed in time. That which comprises rhythm's particular distinctive qualities, its aesthetic value, is the *ordered articulation of elements in their passing in time*, i.e. a certain *regular pattern* in the movement of these elements.

If we are talking about the rhythm of a song or dance, this means that we are talking about a regular movement through time made by particular constituent elements of this song, this dance. In music and poetry the laws governing this movement have to some extent already been considered and studied; theoretical bases for musical composition and metrics—bases which are important for these arts' techniques—have been drawn up. The rhythm of dance has been less well studied. Analytical study of techniques in these fields of art inevitably deals with effective and active movement of the constituent parts which form the particular rhythm.

For this reason, to distinguish it from the rhythm of which we shall be speaking below, let us call the rhythm of these fields of art *active-dynamic rhythm.*

Let us now turn to the plastic arts.

Let us consider a very simple example: a curve depicted on a plane. This curve is likewise imbued with a determinate rhythm. The particular constituent parts of the curve are the various positions of the point as it moves in a specific direction. Consequently, here too we take into account the element of movement; here too it

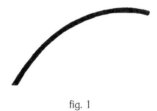

fig. 1

is to do with a certain regular passage of the constituent elements. And here too what is important is not the particular absolute position of the point, but its relation to the previous and following positions—the continuity of the impression which is made by this movement.

In this way, in this case too, we have to do with all the particularities of the rhythm described above. However, there is an important difference between the present case and the previous ones.

In the case of a song or dance the movement of the elements was active; each new element made its appearance only when the previous one was disappearing, while remaining in our consciousness. Here, however, in the formation of a plastic form of whatever kind, the new element is merely added to the old, to the previous element; and the latter does not exist in our minds, but rather occupies a particular place in space.

The feeling of rhythm is here created by the relation between elements which exist in reality, by their simultaneous existence.

The line that has been drawn is the result of the progressive movement of the point as it changes its position in space. But since the line has been depicted, its movement has already ceased and for us, who are looking at the drawn curve, there is no clear sense of perceiving active movement. Nevertheless, we get a certain feeling of rhythm from the curve in question—and consequently the element of movement must exist. And indeed the rhythmic charm that derives from the given curve has its explanation in the fact that each time we look at the curve, we mentally repeat the progressive movement of the point, which once indeed performed this active movement.

If when looking at this curve we take into account its rhythm, this means that in our minds there must necessarily take place a reflection of the original movement of the line's formation—and perhaps so quickly and unconsciously that we are unable to keep track of this in each particular case.

Here there is no active movement of the elements, but what takes place is a certain reflected, passive passage of these elements; and this passage is not impeded by the simultaneous existence of the entire trajectory of this movement. *What we have here is a rhythm that is static* or, as we may call it in a desire to indicate its dynamic pattern—which manifests itself only in our minds—*passive-dynamic.*

An invariable condition of active-dynamic rhythm is fluctuation in time. How we feel this rhythm changes fundamentally depending on the duration of each element and on the position in time of each of the preceding elements. The concept of time is a category that engenders the particular character of the active-dynamic rhythm.

In static rhythm, on the other hand, the concept of time plays a role that is latent and almost entirely inconspicuous. Under certain conditions, we may simultaneously perceive and survey all the elements in a given work.*

The notion of *time* is here replaced by the notion of the *extent* of each constituent element; the latter, however, is nevertheless a function of time.

The *temporal* relation is replaced by a *spatial* succession of elements and by their mutual existence, an existence which is different in each particular case.

The boundaries of each constituent element of active-dynamic rhythm are its temporal extent and number of temporal fluctuations.

The boundaries of the constitutive element of static rhythm, on the other hand, are its spatial extent.

Each of the constituent elements of this rhythm should occupy a determinate and more or less extensive space and should have its own material boundaries, which act upon our visual perceptions.

An interesting example of the combination of the two types of rhythm is ballet, the art of dance. Each particular instant of the dance, each position or "pas" taken or performed by the dancing figure is a static rhythm since it is a function of extent, like any spatial form. The entire combination of such positions, i.e. that which constitutes this dance, is a function of time and thus is an active-dynamic rhythm.

*) The limited size of the work of art or its being situated at a sufficient distance from our eyes.

Dance has such a substantial rhythmic charm because its rhythm combines all the characteristics of the plastic and tonal arts, materialising a rhythm which is complex, being temporal and extensive at the same time.

III.

Thus it is utterly self-evident that in examining the plastic arts—and in particular, the art of architecture—we shall be dealing exclusively with passive-dynamic or static rhythm.

Let us look in more detail at specific characteristics of this rhythm.

Above, we took into account the existence of static rhythm in the drawing of a curve. Let us move now to more complex shapes. Let us look at a two-dimensional rectangle (fig. 2).

We may view the rectangle too as the result of the movement of a point—as the trajectory of the constituent element of this shape. Consequently, in this sense we have to do with a typical example of static rhythm. The only difference is that after beginning its journey in one place, the moving main element arrives at the end of its path [back] in its initial position. This is a characteristic of every spatial shape.* But what constitutes the essence of this or that particular rhythm of an enclosed spatial shape?

*) It should be said that in the same way that a two-dimensional shape is the result of the movement of a point, all spatial [three-dimensional] shapes are the result of the movement of some other element. For instance, a cylinder, cone, and so on are the result of the revolution of a straight line around an axis. Consequently, the same analysis might be transferred from the plane to three-dimensional space. For simplicity's sake, however, we shall continue looking not at spatial shapes, but at projections of these shapes, i.e. two-dimensional images.

fig. 2

When we examine the given rectangle, we see that in three places along its path the moving constituent element changes its direction of movement. The points where the change of direction occurs in the present example are, like the character of the change of direction, not incidental, but are governed by a certain law of movement, which is not difficult to define. This law, in the present case, amounts to the fact that, while the point moves in a particular direction, its trajectory twice forms a similar movement; the point performs a certain *repetition* of its movement. The first instance occurs in the horizontal direction; the second, in the vertical direction. Thus parallel lines are created.

That which constitutes the rhythmic character of this shape consists precisely of this sense of regular repetition. Our eye, perceiving the same movement for a second time, feels a certain relief because the movement is already familiar to it. The energy initially expended in perceiving this or that movement is expended in a lesser quantity when it is perceived for a second time. Our eye to some extent relaxes when it perceives a movement which has already been laid down in the mind, and the rhythmic feeling consists in the same movement being laid down but with a minimal expenditure of energy, reinforcing and deepening the feeling which was originally received, a feeling which is the result of a 'nervous current' moving from the periphery to the centre. The passage of the 'current' leaves a more or less deep trace in the brain. If subsequently a new 'current' analogous to the first passes from the same peripheral receiver to the centre, the first trace is deepened. The traces of these feelings build up in the brain, magnifying the initial strength of the irritation. On the other hand, by creating a particular sequence in perception of feelings, (since whatever kind the rhythm is, the element of movement in it is inevitable), the rhythmic feeling to a certain extent eliminates the simultaneity of action of different irritations.*

Thus if we wanted to depict merely the rhythmic manifestation of the given form, putting to one side, so to speak, all its other characteristics, we should act as follows: we should depict two pairs of parallel lines (vertical and horizontal). The *repetitiveness of movement* in these parallel lines constitutes the rhythmic essence of the rectangle. This element of repetition, due to its significance, determines two other principal characteristics of this shape: the equality of the parallel sections of line and the straightness and evenness of the corners that are formed.

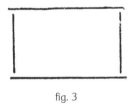

fig. 3

*) Fechner's Law says: "In order that there should be a feeling, it is necessary that the irritation should possess a certain minimal strength, since should this not be the case, the 'threshold' of our consciousness will not be passed." Weber's Law says that the lower the "threshold", the fewer are the irritations acting simultaneously on our nervous system.

The ease with which we comprehend the laws governing formation of the given shape explains to us the rhythmic quality of its perception.

Of course, the law of repetition does not exhaust the precise determination of shape. Also of primary importance is the differing length of these parallel movements. The rectangle may have different proportions, ranging from the regular square to the endlessly elongated thin rectangle.

The artistic content of these shapes, of course, will differ. Consequently, in addition to the law regarding repetitiveness of movement, also of significance for the given shape, is the relation of the absolute sizes of the trajectories between the instants when the direction of the movement changes, i.e. a certain *harmonious* state of form. Although this harmony is a concept of a different kind, since it is not directly related to dynamism of form, it nevertheless, being in the final analysis a function of movement, may be classified as a circumstantial constituent element of the feeling of rhythm.

It is indeed the case that the harmoniousness of the given shape derives from the fact that it has been formed in a certain regular way and thus has the objective of making the given shape easier for us to grasp in our minds. This is also the immediate objective of rhythm. However, while in rhythm the regular formation derives from the *quality* of the movement (direction), in harmony it is more static and its essence is exhausted by the *quantity* (mathematical content) of the movement.

Let us compare, for instance, two rectangles.

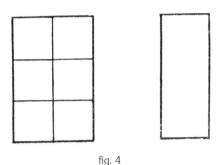

fig. 4

Both rectangles have an identical rhythmic formation, but at the same time their perceived characters are different. It is not difficult to see that the reason for this lies in the different mathematical relation between the absolute sizes of the sections. While in one rectangle the ratio between the sides is not explained by simple numbers, in the other the sides relate to one another in the ratio 2:3. Which is to say that apart from the rhythmic regularity which is common to both figures, one of the rectangles possesses an additional numerical regularity which facilitates even more the quickness and painlessness of our perceptions, i.e. a certain harmonious quality of form.

In this way, while the rhythm of the spatial shape expresses the regularity of its dynamic formation, the harmony of the form specifies this regularity in a particular mathematical relation, i.e. *harmony is the mathematical essence of rhythm.*

We may exhaustively convey the rhythmic content of the given rectangle by means of just two definitions:

1) a definition of a certain regular repetitiveness of the direction of movement of the constituent element, and

2) the mathematical relation between the absolute sizes of the trajectories of movement when the direction

of the movement changes, i.e. the harmonic content of the given shape.

The former is a quality that is specifically rhythmic; the second is derivative, extremely important from the point of view of form, but mainly determines qualities which are only functionally dependent on the dynamic principle.

Thus the element of repetitiveness is an essential part of static rhythm. This means that after a certain spatial interval the direction of movement of the constituent element is repeated.

The existence of this spatial interval is necessary because, if there were no such interval, the direction of movement would not be repeated but would coincide with the previous movement; consequently, we may represent the repetitiveness of the static rhythm in a certain *alternation* of the trajectories of movement with spatial gaps or intervals.

In the case of our two-dimensional rectangle we have to do with a certain alternation of the lines of movement with spatial intervals—and, moreover, to an identical extent in the horizontal and vertical directions. But that which is barely graspable within the scope of depiction of an enclosed spatial form is especially clearly revealed, as we shall see subsequently, in the coordination of an entire group of architectural forms. The repetitiveness of elements is grasped here too only in that they follow one another in a certain regular succession and, as before, the more rhythmic the succession of elements, the simpler and clearer is the law that determines how they follow one another.

IV.

Let us look at the curve shown in the drawing below. This curve is also the result of the movement of a point along a specific trajectory. It is easy to see that in relation

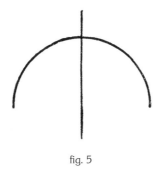

fig. 5

to a particular vertical line drawn in the plane of the point's movement, its movement is repeated, but in the opposite order. Here too we have to do with a certain rhythm of repetitiveness, but one which is slightly different from that described above. The entire essence of this rhythm is a matter of the fact that what is happening here is a kind of augmentation of movement up to the vertical line that has been drawn, after which the movement is repeated with a gradual diminishment. Moreover, the laws of augmentation and diminution are precisely identical.

We here have to do with the well-known phenomenon of symmetry—and the vertical line is precisely an axis of symmetry. This makes it clear that the law of symmetry too is a function of repetition, in just the same way as the law of alternation.

If we turn to the above rectangles, we see that they too contain elements of symmetry.

In general, we may say that repetition, alternation of elements, or symmetry of a spatial form are signs that the form complies with a simple rhythmic law of one kind or another.

The rhythmic charm of symmetrical shapes has its explanation in the basic psycho-physiological characteristics of our sense of sight. Each of our two eyes perceives all shapes separately, and yet the image which is formed in each eye is converse to the image which forms in the other eye, just as many parts of our body—ears, hands, and legs—are converse in relation to one another.

In this way our idea of a shape is formed in our minds only following the formation of two repeated, but converse, i.e. symmetrical feelings in both eyes. We may say that our vision itself is symmetrical in relation to an imaginary axis that may notionally be drawn between the eyes.

The same principle is the basis for the stereoscope: each eye perceives a separate idea of the shape which has already been prepared on paper, and the idea [formed by one eye] is the converse [of the idea formed by the other], with the two ideas being strictly symmetrical to one another with regard to an axis running between the eyes.

The element of converse repetition already occurs in our minds, which is why the charm of the rhythm of symmetry is so strong given that perception of this rhythm has already been prepared by the physiological structure of the eyes. The feelings perceived by our organ of sense and accumulated in our brain, are made available to our imagination, whose functioning is extremely individual. We may identify two main means by which the imagination disposes of the feelings it receives. The first means is reproductive, while the second is constructive. The reproductive means is the more mechanical and is rarely to be found in a pure form since the work of perception is undoubtedly a creative process. For the most part, our imagination breaks down ideas into their main elements and builds images, instinctively stylising them and correcting external perceptions in accordance with the requirements of its own physiological structure; and since the main factor in visual sensations is the eyes, it consequently corrects them in accordance with the physiological make-up of the eyes; in other words, the constructive means of disposing of our sensations is the more creative and imparts symmetry to images of the external world. Were the human organ of vision not two symmetrical eyes, but a single eye, then symmetry would undoubtedly not exist as a means of physiological impact. That is why this rhythm is such an important element of the plastic arts and in particular of architecture.

And when the architect or jaded stylist in ancient times depicted a particular shape, he in the great majority of cases constructed symmetrical volumes, i.e. instinctively followed the laws of rhythm, the laws which make the most economical use of our energy of perception.

And indeed, all particular architectural images—be they elements of the mass of the architectural massif or an architectural/decorative motif—are always symmetrical. The way in which these images are coordinated may be subject to a particular kind of rhythm, but each element on its own is the product of an extremely simple rhythm, a rhythm of the most organic kind—the rhythm of symmetry. And the entire history of architecture provides us with endless examples of this. Even in Romanesque or Gothic architecture (not to mention Classical architecture), where the individualisation of particular decorative architectural elements is taken to the furthest extreme, we inevitably find in each element an axis of symmetry and have no difficulty in sensing the rhythmic enchantment of the simplest laws of symmetry. However complex and however grotesque its intertwining of images from the animal and vegetative worlds, the design of the capital always strives to settle in our minds and is always subject to the laws of symmetrical rhythm. The entire *modenature* of the capital, the base, and shaft—everything invariably has its own axis of symmetry.

The rhythm of symmetry, that rhythm which is the most organic and most simple, is the favourite rhythm of the enclosed three-dimensional architectural form.

V.

Let us look at the two groups of figures depicted in the drawings below. It is very easy to see that the rhythms of the first pair of figures are imbued with the same kindred spirit. The shades of rhythmic feeling generated by the different ratio of the absolute sizes of the trajectories of movement (their harmonious essence) are easily smoothed over in our minds if we turn to the figures in the *second* row.

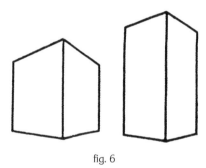

fig. 6

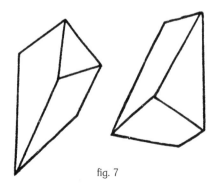

fig. 7

As clearly and painlessly as the first row settles into place in our minds, so the figures in the second pair rapidly cut through our minds and each time in a different way. Our psycho-physical reaction usually consists of two elements:

1) perception of a sensation and

2) assimilation of this sensation by our organism.

During both assimilation and perception, figures of the first order make use of the category of repetition, which facilitates both these processes. Figures of the second order, however, achieve the element of perception by means of direct irritation, a feeling which can often be very intense. But the stronger the element of perception, the more complex and prolonged is the element of assimilation. The energy expended on comprehending this group of figures considerably exceeds the energy needed for assimilation of the first pair. Not merely in moving from one figure in the second order to the other, but also in perceiving movement within the bounds of just one of these figures, we feel no peace of mind. Each new direction of the trajectory is unexpected for us and disrupts the inertia that has already begun to form as a result of movement in one direction. Looking at these figures, our ability to perceive is constantly strained and these movements not only do not unconsciously leave a settled impression in our memories, but are even difficult to assimilate when we make an effort to recall them.

While we experience a feeling of sympathy towards the first group, with regard to the second group we find in ourselves a certain hostility, which has to be overcome in order for us to assimilate the perceptions. In distinction to the figures in the first group, we shall call these figures *arrhythmic*. They contain no regular repetition or regular alternation of elements; they possess no symmetry: a simple and clear law of movement is missing from them.

Of course, for this group too we may find a law of movement, but this law, even when comprehended, will always be complex and an effort, sometimes a very great effort, will be required in order for it to settle in our minds.

In as much as any curve may have its own equation of movement, and in as much as any spatial figure can have its own law of formation, just so there are no arrhythmic shapes at all.

However, the criterion—which for us, of course is always relative—will be a certain element of simplicity and clarity of the law describing the movement of the constituent element during formation of this or that shape. Thus it would be more correct to say that figures in the first group are more rhythmic than figures in the second group. However, due to the dynamic pattern of the way in which the latter form is more alien to us, less comprehensible, more complex, we therefore put these figures in a special group under the name "arrhythmic figures".

Nevertheless, such shapes are to be found in the form of particular images or compositional aggregations in works belonging to the plastic arts. Moreover, their arrhythmic quality is even sometimes deliberately emphasised, constituting a kind of formal objective. The artist wishes to compel us to expend the maximum amount of energy in perception; he wants to force us to look for a law describing the rhythm in this apparent lack of rhythm.

And sometimes in this intense work of overcoming and looking there is more sensual pleasure than in perceptions that are clearly rhythmic, since the viewer in this case is more involved in the process of creation. That which is achieved with difficulty acquires more value.

But in any case, lack of rhythm, as a problem of rhythm, constitutes a category of perceptions which is distinct from purely rhythmic perceptions, the laws governing whose assimilation are clear and distinct.

VI.

The main laws describing the formation of the architectural mass and the laws of rhythm which animate this mass are extremely simple. They are almost always laws for the formation of a regular geometric shape and are clear in their mathematical essence and distinct in their rhythm.

It would hardly be inaccurate to say that the great multiplicity of the main architectural masses—our artistic and historical baggage—is exhausted by the parallelepiped, the straight line, the pyramid, the cone, and sections of a spherical surface.

Moreover, the five latter geometric bodies are to be found relatively less often and for the most part as subsidiary shapes while the most common architectural form remains to the present day the parallelepiped—which sometimes extends more in a horizontal direction, sometimes extends more in a vertical direction, and sometimes takes the clearly regular shape of the cube.

Even prehistoric architecture, notwithstanding the limited means available to the primeval architect, demonstrates to us almost all these shapes in a primitive form. Man's first creation was perhaps the vertically placed parallelepiped slab of a more or less regular shape. Here we for the first time encounter man's need to reveal the vertical forces of architecture.

The modest menhir is in essence the first conductor of one of the conflicting principles to be found in any work of great architecture. With the planting of a vertical, there appeared the first active principle of architecture—

fig. 8

the first opposition between the creative 'I' and the endless horizontal of the universe. This was the beginning of a great conflict in which the creative face of art is always revealed.

And a long time later, when man has learned to conquer this element of conflict in his unrivalled monuments, he still from time to time plants this vertical in the ground as a soaring symbol of the active energy of the creator. Alongside the horizontally extensive masses of churches he has never forgotten to place the vertical of the bell-tower; and in the history of architecture there was a time when a wave of northern peoples developed this mutinous, unreliable, and impetuous feeling of verticality to its final logical extreme, covering almost all of Europe in it and creating the restless and impudent art of the Gothic style, art which stands as a separate and astonishing enigma in the midst of the boundless path of human progress. But even in the menhir we see an attempt by the architect to slightly mitigate the conflict, to reinforce and link the planted vertical with the land. And indeed the architect chooses stones which

fig. 9

are wider and more compact at the bottom and thus make an impression of greater stability and greater connection with the horizontal of the ground. This is the prototype of the pyramid; it is a pyramid which is as yet excessively elongated, like an Egyptian obelisk. In this way we see a new type of vertical being established— one which is wider towards the bottom, more stable, and extremely viable due to the way in which its inner feeling of alleviation of the tension of the vertical is combined with the rationality of the laws of statics. And indeed this is the kind of silhouette that is most often seen in vertical structures of all kinds such as bell-towers, towers, or even Gothic cathedrals.

We see the same feeling of alleviation of tension, only more intense, in the Egyptian pyramid. In the pyramid there is much less verticality manifested than in the menhir. The architect understands all the importance which is possessed for his art by forces that are horizontal, tranquil, balanced, and reflect the cosmic majesty of the universe. Admittedly, here too there is an element of conflict, but of conflict that is resolved; and, as a symbol of pacification,

fig. 10

we find a gently sloped incline which is equal in effect to a horizontal and vertical—an incline which we later encounter in the pediment of the Greek temple.

But a true dynamic collision in architecture is manifested by the rhythm of the dolmen (a horizontal slab placed over two vertical slabs). Here we for the first time encounter a striving to encompass space and enclose it with an architectural mass; we encounter what is perhaps man's first house—a deliberate manifestation of horizontal and vertical forces. This is the first abstraction from an experience of space understood as a product of impulses deriving from man.

We for the first time encounter a spreading of space into depth, width, and height; we encounter a mathematical determination of space in its multiplicity of three dimensions. We have here a parallelepiped (as yet bounded only on four sides) encompassing space. Rising off the earth, the architect of the dolmen thus established once again—as in the case of the menhir, only much more distinctly—a hostile collision between gravitational attraction and a striving towards space.

The two vertical slabs are placed in a monumental fashion on the ground; the third, horizontal slab lies

fig. 11

on top of them. The vertical slabs point into space, but the horizontal slab lying on top of them limits them and restrains them in a particular volume. From here it is only one step to the parallelepiped encompassing space on all six sides, i.e. to the true human house. Particular aspects of this conflict determine the particular harmony of the mass of the parallelepiped/house.

When the striving into space prevails, when vertical forces prevail, this creates the vertically elongated parallelepipeds of modern skyscrapers with all the tension of their rhythm.

When the pull towards the ground—i.e. horizontal forces—prevails, this gives rise to the lengthwise spreading seen in the parallelepipeds of ancient culture—parallelepipeds which pacify, balance, and reconcile you with the world.

In both cases a three-dimensional form of indisputable regularity is created—a shape which has straight corners and parallel lines. *The regular, encompassing parallelepiped is the basis and prototype of the great majority of architectural monuments.*

fig. 12

But even in prehistoric architecture we encounter also a different understanding of space—as an unstable and fickle substance surrounding man. This is space in which all the directions are of equal value, based on the mathematical principle of the homogeneity and continuity of space.

This is also one of the first structures belonging to prehistoric man: a circular ring of separately standing stones called a cromlech.

Here we find an entirely different understanding of mass and a completely different approach to the latter's forms. While in the dolmen we see a firm basis for the acceptance of volume as three dimensions—we have a distinct feeling of three-dimensional space—in the cromlech we encounter an illusory feeling of space, a feeling which is false and deceptive. Our eyes find nothing to support them in the determining of volume, no starting points—since they are encompassed by unsteady matter which radiates in an absolutely identical fashion in different directions. In the parallelepiped we find a distinct and accurate impression of the dimensions of the volume, but in the cylindrical cromlech we are always being led astray; the volumes of the space seem to us to be larger than they are in actual fact, due to the fact we have no reliable sensations by which to orient ourselves.

The rhythm of circular shapes gives us the illusion of volume whereas the rhythm of straight shapes gives a more accurate indication of them.

From the perforated cylinder of the cromlech it is just one step to the voluminous cylinder of the circular buildings that have often been built by man. Further development of such cylindrical structures is to be found in spherical surfaces covering circular buildings such as the Pantheon, in the same way that rectangular structures are covered by various kinds of pyramids or prisms.

The cone-shaped mass, which is sometimes found as a subsidiary form, likewise has its prototype in prehistoric architecture—namely, in prehistoric burial mounds.

The regular polygonal prism probably came into existence as a shape transitional between straight and circular shapes and was used mainly as a transition in the topmost parts of the architectural concept.

But, of course, the great art of architecture, which in its enchanting diversity does not confine itself to the simple shapes listed above, creates an entire array of complex shape formations.

However, closer examination of these shapes convinces us that, with a very few exceptions, all these complex monuments of architecture derive their main masses from combinations of the simple geometric bodies which we have considered.

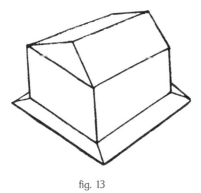

fig. 13

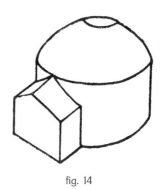

fig. 14

For instance, any Greek temple, considered as a pattern of masses, constitutes a combination of three geometric bodies—a truncated pyramid (the stylobate), a parallelepiped (the body of the cella), and a trihedral prism (the roof). The Pantheon in Rome is a combination of a cylinder, part of the surface of a sphere, and the parallelepiped and prism of the portico. Any Romanesque church consists of a considerably more complex combination of the same simple bodies. Here we see a multiplicity of parallelepipeds, prisms, pyramids, and curved surfaces.

In Gothic architecture these main masses are multiplied to form architectural molecules that are repeated many times, feverishly and tensely soaring upwards.

We find a kind of disruption of this regularity and simplicity of principal masses in Baroque architecture, which floods the entire building with an endlessly flowing corporeal substance. Here there is no longer anything of the fragmentation of Gothic architecture. Using simple forms, Baroque strips them of sharp edges and corners, bends them, and inflates them, so to speak, with matter, creating a complex curving of planes and lines.

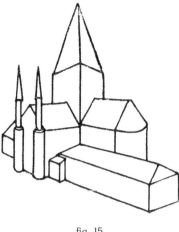

fig. 15

However, here too we remain for the most part within the boundaries of shapes that are symmetrical and regular—and only the especial tension of Baroque's rhythm leads it to these deviations.

VII.

Such are the main issues to do with rhythm in the formation of architectural mass and in the revelation of this mass' general outline. But in each particular architectural monument, and in its progressive formal fulfilment, the main task breaks up into a multiplicity of individual rhythmic problems and integrates the general sensation of a perception in a multitude of particular rhythmic fluctuations.

Let us compare the curve in the drawing below with a series of similar curves. We can easily see that while in the first curve the rhythm is merely indicated in a schematic way, in the series it manifests itself distinctly and in sharp focus. In looking for the reason for this phenomenon we should, above all, turn to the main function of rhythm—the element of repetition.

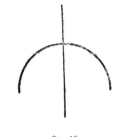

fig. 16

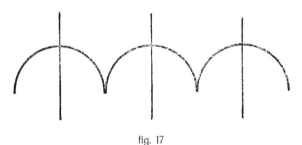

fig. 17

And indeed we notice that in the series of these curves repetition is manifested much more clearly, as a result of which the main cause of the feeling of rhythm and of our attitude of 'sympathy' towards it is reinforced and becomes deeper and firmer.

Here we have not just one repetition but several, each of which makes it easier for us to perceive the following and at the same time intensifies the feeling of rhythm.

From the main element of repetition derive, as we already know, the remaining qualities of rhythm.

Thus the following conclusion naturally follows from this example: the larger the number of elements in a particular rhythmic group, the clearer and more distinct the feeling of rhythm which is generated by these elements.

The same reflections may be applied to the field of spatial forms also. Whereas in an individual architectural element we already feel a rhythmic quality, we cannot not be aware that here, in addition to the dynamic pattern of rhythm itself, a significant role is played by rhythm's functional qualities—i.e. symmetrical formation and mathematical essence (harmony). The artistic significance of the individual spatial form—whether it be a mass or a particular architectural element, such as, for instance, a column—is absolutely exhausted by not just the dynamic pattern of its rhythm, but also its static qualities. If we look at an entire group of spatial forms, here there cannot be fluctuations in determination of its artistic essence. The rhythmic charm coming from this group is wholly and exclusively dependent on the dynamic pattern of these elements, on the regularity of their spatial progression and the depth to which they penetrate our consciousness, which depth condenses and reinforces our perceptions. Whatever work of architecture we examine, from the most simple to the most complex, the self-evident quality of this rhythmic enchantment encompassed in it will become clear. The architectural skeleton, in which naked matter alternates with the vacancies of intervals (windows and doors), in itself constitutes all the endless capacity of this or that rhythmic manifestation, for in it we may be enchanted by a particular melody of alternations or a particular recitative of repetitions. In blocks of matter, in the undiluted tectonics of forms where there is not even a barely noticeable striving for decorativeness or for fragmented articulation of elements, we often find a true feeling of rhythm. The might of the stone, the clear and strong energy of the architectural matter, an energy which is manifested in images stated with such restraint, alternates with gaping spaces; there is not a single superfluous sound, not a single hint of other possibilities. At the same time, what an endless rhythmic enchantment sometimes streams from these architectural bodies, which are simultaneously bound fast in their perfection and subject to endless movement materialised by the dynamic pattern of their rhythm.

However, as far back as in the most ancient times, the primeval architect, not content with this most simple means of rhythmic influence, felt the need to create an independent organism—a pillar, pylon, or column—capable of serving as a powerful conductor of rhythmic ideas. The Classical order, as an aggregate of repeated shafts of columns, is just as instinctive as the conscious need for a rhythmic manifestation of the architect's creative instincts, a need which led to the formation of the concept of the columned portico or temple.

One pair of columns gives almost no feeling of rhythm; it brings the eye to a stop on the axis between them and beautifully frames the motif that is enclosed by them; but since it frames and *stops* the gaze, this means that it does not provide the rhythm with sufficient force and conviction.

fig. 18

Three columns possess the same quality, since they make it possible to place on the line of the middle column an axis which catches and holds our attention. This is true of the monument of Thrasyllus (fourth century BC), where on top of the central column a sculptural portrait has been placed. The Greeks were highly aware of this, and we find almost not a single temple or single structure with two or three columns. There is a vase fresco from the fourth century BC that depicts a scene from the tragedy *Iphigenia in Tauris*. Here we see something like a pavilion or temple with two columns on the side with the pediment. But in the middle is a depiction of Iphigenia and the role of these columns is not dynamic, but static—to bring our attention to a stop on this depiction.*

fig. 19

*) This is precisely the point of ancient steles, which are often embellished with two columns or pilasters.

Four columns already possess clear qualities of the dynamic impact of rhythm, and indeed we quite often find four-columned structures in ancient art. Examples are: the temple of the wingless Nike (Athenae Nices) in the Acropolis in Athens; the Treasure House of the Knidians in Delphi (middle of the sixth century BC); and the northern portico of the Erechtheion (fifth century BC).

There are no five-columned temples—and no temples in general with an odd number of columns, since there would then always be the shaft of a column in their middle, as opposed to a gap—and this makes it impossible to place the main entrance in the centre of the temple.*

On the other hand, Greek architects' favourite number of columns was six—and indeed most temples are six-columned.

Examples are: the Temple of Concordia in Agrigento (end of the fifth century BC); the Temple of Poseidon in

fig. 20

*) The exception is the Temple of the Giants in Agrigento, where the rear-end facade has seven columns and the front-end facade has six; the middle column has been omitted and replaced with a vacant passage leading to the central door.

Paestum, a most perfect temple; the Temple of Aphaia on Aegina; the Temple of Theseus; the temple in Selinunte; and a great number of others.

Indeed, the number 'six' contains a kind of enigmatic magic of rhythmic enchantment. In six repeated column shafts there is an amazing triumph of the architect's rhythmic might. These six columns are sufficiently forceful in establishing rhythmic regularity and at the same time do not transport our minds too far, do not put our minds to sleep to such an extent that our eyes lose the strength and might of the unity of the overall concept.

But when in the the fifth century BC, the golden age of Pericles, Phidias, Iktinos, and Callicrates wanted to create something out of the ordinary, something stunning—wanted to create the Pathenon which was to become a grand and endlessly perfect landmark of the human genius—they naturally had the desire to reinforce and deepen the rhythmic feeling, and they turned the temple into an eight-columned one. In this we see amazing instinct

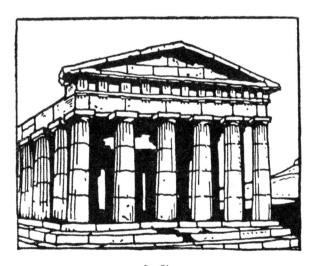

fig. 21

and a precise evaluation of the role of rhythm in the work of architecture, the apogee of the purely musical dynamic might of the architect, the heyday of the Greek genius, but… in this there is also to be seen the first step towards decline.

Let us compare the Temple of Poseidon in Paestum or any other six-columned temple with the Parthenon. To the extent that the Parthenon is more rhythmic, more musical, and more appreciably dynamic, to the same extent the Temple of Poseidon is more mighty, more resilient, and more architectural because the force of the architect's creativity is not only in establishing rhythm, but also in the ability to overcome it.

The unity of impression of and the integrity of the overall concept of perfect ancient monuments is the result of understanding the objectives and limits of the effect of the dynamic laws of rhythm.

Rhythm of the kind which prolongs its movement endlessly and continuously tends in the best examples of architecture to be established only in secondary parts of the architectural concept, but it is usually the case that this is where the rhythm of the main motif comes from, and this rhythm is more enclosed and determinate, not merely indicating a certain *rhythmic* quality, but creating a perfect and *unmoving* coordination of individual elements.

And indeed the majority of Greek temples have six columns on their main facades while their side facades may have as many as 17 columns. It is characteristic that it is only in the Macedonian age, the age of the decline of the Greek style, that we encounter the temple in Miletus with ten columns on the principal facade.

Thus it is clear that in the group of architectural elements an increase in the number of elements likewise increases the strength of the feeling of rhythm; however,

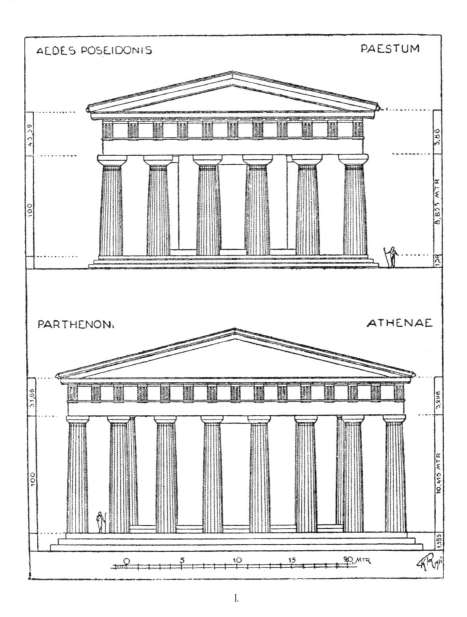

AEDES POSEIDONIS   PAESTUM

PARTHENON,   ATHENAE

I.

beyond a certain limit, the strength of the rhythm that has been attained has a destructive effect on the integrity and unity of the architectural concept.

VIII.

In works of architecture the most primitive rhythmic manifestation of the will of the architect is achieved by the repetition of some elementary architectural form.

An example might be the prehistoric cromlech, i.e. the rhythmic ring of uniformly placed parallelepiped pillars.*

This is a manifestation of architectural rhythm in its purest and simplest form. Rhythm of this kind may be called *simple rhythm*.

But in its further development architecture becomes increasingly complex and the same rhythmic laws are materialised not in simple forms, but in complex combinations of these forms and by the coexistence of a large number of artistic elements. And whereas in the example of the cromlech examined above the rhythmic unit or beat, so to speak, the *module of rhythm*, was the simple parallelepiped pillar, in the majority of architectural monuments the rhythmic beat is a complex group of forms. We may call this kind of rhythm *complex rhythm*.

The completed development of an architectural order is an example of this kind of rhythm. Here what happens is so-called "integration": the particular constituent parts are united to create an idea of the whole in our minds. The individual constituent parts of the rhythm coordinate with one another in order to create a single whole feeling of complex rhythm. Like integration of the word in poetry, we find ourselves constantly encountering integration of rhythm in complex formations.

Let us look at how this kind of integration of architectural rhythm is realised in the Doric temple with which we are already familiar. What is the rhythmic

* Of more or less parallelepiped shape.

module in this temple? At first sight, it would seem to be only the column. However, closer inspection reveals to us that it is not just the column on its own, but the entire vertical section of the order, from the board of the stylobate to the mutules of the cornice, which forms a complex rhythmic beat. Of course, when form is put to one side, things here are the same as in the case of the prehistoric cromlech; moreover, in every work of architecture the module of rhythm is the ideal axis of symmetry which is rhythmically repeated and alternates with spatial intervals. And in this sense all rhythms will be simple. But this kind of abstract examination does not exhaust reality. In architecture we always see this ideal unit of rhythm materialised; we always see this axis of symmetry constantly passing through a certain material form, or, to be more accurate, through an entire complex group of individual material forms. And in this sense architecture almost always involves complex rhythms.

In the Doric temple that we looked at the main element of rhythm is the shaft of the column. But here we should consider a range of *additional* rhythmic elements that are integrated in a unified feeling of complex rhythm. These additional rhythms, always subordinate to the main rhythm, may be arranged both at the top of the axis of symmetry and on both sides of this axis, i.e. vertically and horizontally.

In the frieze of the Doric order we encounter a motif called the "triglyph", whose axis coincides with the axis of the column: this is the most important of the elements of additional rhythm in the Doric order. The triglyph is divided at the bottom from the architrave and at the top from the cornice by shelves. And on both sides of it, vertically, we find new elements of additional rhythm—

above, a strongly projecting "mutule", and below, a weakly projecting shelf. But both elements are situated strictly on the main axis of the column and in this way underline their subordination to the main rhythm.*

These are all *elements of additional rhythm in a vertical direction.*

Careful examination will convince us of the existence of numerous additional rhythms on both sides of the main axis too. In the shaft of the column we see a number of vertical grooves, which are symmetrical with regard to the same axis and, finally, under the mutules and the bottom shelf we notice a large number of *guttae* which are likewise arranged symmetrically with regard to the main columnal axis.** All these are *elements of additional rhythm in a horizontal direction.*

But what role is played by all these elements of horizontal and vertical additional rhythm? What is their rhythmic function and how do they enrich the essence of the complex rhythm?

Let us recall simple rhythm, the rhythm of the cromlech: pillar after pillar are repeated, each time leaving an impression in our minds, but the rhythmic essence of the pillar itself is so simple that the eye does not dwell for long on it and moves on. The rhythmic sense is superficial, and for this reason its charm too is not so strong. This is a simple melody played on a shepherd's pipe.

Now let us look at the Doric temple. Column after column are repeated in our minds, leaving in them a

---

*) The exception is the corner triglyphs in the Greco-Doric order, which are slightly displaced from the axis of the column in order to fill the corner of the frieze. The Romans refrained from repeating this rhythmic irregularity, leaving the corner of the frieze free.

**) Cannelures.

feeling of rhythm. But our eyes linger on the column. The additional rhythms draw our gaze upwards: our eyes run over the triglyph, the shelves, and the mutules. The additional rhythms turn our attention to the sides: our gaze is sated with repetitions of the fluting of the shaft, the grooves of the triglyph, the *guttae*, and the mutules. The same rhythm is slowly, as it conquers our perceptional capacity, filled in in our minds, becoming firmer and deeper to the extent of the capacity of our rhythmic perception. Only then does the sated eye move on, following the path of repetition of both the main and additional elements.

What a difference compared with the cromlech: how much wealth and diversity of rhythmic feeling! Our eyes, even when they linger on a particular element of rhythm, only strengthen in our minds the overall charm of the rhythm. A static halt for an instant in the movement of the rhythm not only does not deprive it of effectiveness, but even deepens it.

The difference between simple and complex rhythm is the same as that between a piece of music in which the element is the individual sound and another piece of music where the rhythmic beat is the chord, an entire consonance of tones which are linked with one another and supplement the charm of the main rhythm.

In this way, integration of rhythm complicates the rhythmic module and thus makes the quality of the rhythm more intense, more forceful. But we have already seen in the rhythm of the Doric portico a series of additional rhythms in a horizontal direction, such as: the fluting of the shaft and the grooves of the triglyphs which, intensifying the rhythm by improving the quality of the beat, at the same time boost its dynamic quality, creating a number of smaller intermediate rhythmic elements.

It is indeed the case that the main quality of rhythm is its dynamic pattern. Thus there naturally arises a need for *continuity of effect* of rhythm. The eye moves from one rhythmic module to another, but it can also stop on the gap between them. It is necessary for this gap to be sufficiently dynamic—for it not to hold attention, but to lightly move that attention on further.

It is necessary for the gap to transmit movement. This need may be especially strongly felt when utilitarian material or purely formal considerations make it impossible to place the axes of symmetry close to one another and necessitate the use of spatially large rhythmic intervals.

On such occasions the architect's genius resorts to rhythm of a different order, which may be called *transmissive rhythm*. A highly expressive manifestation of this rhythm may be seen in numerous rhythmic accessories of the ancient portico such as intermediate elements (elements between columns), including triglyphs, metopes, and other decorative motifs of the frieze.

These elements, whose axes of symmetry are situated between the main axes, create a rhythmic transfer of movement.

At the same time, they possess the special recitative enchantment of a simple succession of sounds backing up in song the power of the complex chords of the main rhythmic elements.

In those cases when the frieze of a portico is lacking in these transmissive elements (i.e. in the Ionic order), Greek architects used a sculptural frieze—a spatially continuous frieze whose lines of bodily movements and folds of figures' clothes sing again the main melody of the rhythm.

These rhythms are usually placed in the top part of the composition (the entablature), which gives them a certain importance of effect, but their quality is always very simple and even primitive compared to the main rhythms (both with respect to linear composition and with respect to depth and clarity of relief) because were this not so, they could compete with them and, instead of continuity of dynamic pattern, a danger of new static moments would arise. The sounds of the recitative are clear and distinct: they should manifest all the purity of unadorned melody. Their artistic effect is the same as the effect of several simple sounds linking complex combinations in a series of elegant chords; the purity and clarity of these transmissive sounds ensure the continuity of rhythmic movement of the musical work.

The same requirement for continuity of the effect of rhythm created another variety of rhythm, which we shall call *connective*.

The simplest form of this rhythm is arches connecting pillars. Here we have complete fluidity of effect and continuity of rhythmic feeling. The main element of rhythm transitions—gently, gradually, growing and diminishing in the rise and fall of the arch—to another element. Here there is no need for either over-singing or transmission. Here we have direct spatial extensiveness of the dynamic effect. The Greeks, of course, knew about connective rhythm, but without actually employing it. The Greek genius was not so rhythmic as to see the true value of such rhythm. The architect's feeling of rhythm was held in check by the problem of 'spatial harmony', in the resolving of which, the clear and objectively beautiful genius of the Hellenes found its expression.

In this respect the additional and over-singing rhythms of grooves, triglyphs, mutules, and *guttae* perfectly reveal the qualities of the Greeks' feeling of rhythm; in their choice of rhythmic elements the Greeks took care of these qualities' harmonic perfection. It is indeed the case that the articulations of the Doric order form a perfect spatial-compositional pattern, regardless of this pattern's dynamic qualities.

II.

The Romans, on the other hand, who always made extensive use of all formal possibilities and had lost the canonised perfection of the Greek temple, always turned to the arch as a rhythmic instrument, combining it sometimes with elements of the Greek architrave order. This led to the creation of an extremely interesting Roman motif, an outstanding example of which is the

Colosseum, where the columns serve as the principal rhythmic beats, fluidly joined together by the arcs of the arches in the intervals.

fig. 22

However, there is here a degree of imperfection in the lack of consistency in the rhythmic beats and arches of the intervals. And it was only many centuries later, during the age of the late Renaissance in the north of Italy, that the architectural school headed by Sansovino and Palladio came into existence—a school which devoted itself mainly to resolving purely rhythmic problems. It was then that the technique of connective rhythm used in the Flavian amphitheatre was developed to its full perfection.

In the well-known Palladian motif in the basilica in Vicenza the rhythmic beat is enriched with two small columns at the sides. The function of the columns is precisely to act as direct transmitters and links between the main column and the arch.

The forms and proportions of the small column are similar to the large column and our gaze, as it passes from one to the other, does not for a second lose the force of the beat, moving on to the interval before the rhythmic feeling deriving from the module can weaken.* We might say that here the spatial boundary between the beat and the interval—the boundary that constitutes the significant difference between architectural and musical rhythm—is almost eroded and its very quality becomes so full and so directly connected that it reaches the extreme where temporal and spatial rhythms differ little from one another in their physiological effect: the extreme where architecture is in some cases no less musical than the architectural concept for a work of music.

IX.

Let us look at two rhythmic series of elements. The essence of both series is utterly identical. Nevertheless, it is not difficult to see that the rhythmic feeling of the second group is considerably stronger and deeper than the first. This happens for two reasons.

First, the harmonic quality of the rhythm of the second series is more evident to our eyes. In the first series this quality needs to be checked in each particular case and is thus more difficult to perceive. It is indeed the case that when our eyes pass from one element to the other, they must turn for an instant to the previous

*) Likewise, the movement of the sculptural figures of men and women placed above the arches underlines the directness of the transition from one rhythmic beat to the next. (The 'library' by Sansovino.)

element again in order that, by comparing the two, they should convince themselves of the complete equality of value of their spatial dimensions. It is only then that our gaze moves on to the next, new element.

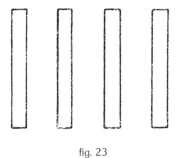

fig. 23

Moreover, each time the same thing happens: our perceptive facility must not just feel a passive satisfaction from the repetition of elements of rhythm, but must also perform the active work of comparing each new element with the previous one. Since extra energy is expended on perception, there is consequently a weakening in the intensity of the feeling of rhythm.

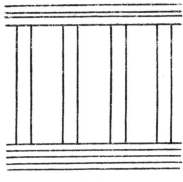

fig. 24

Something utterly different occurs with the process of perception in the second series of elements. The rhythmic beats alternating with the intervals are not free-standing, but are enclosed above and below, spatially constrained, squeezed between two rows of parallel lines. The geometric axiom "sections of parallels between parallel lines are equal" is [here] not just an abstract theorem, but also an extremely convincing one—a visually self-evident truth which is easy for our organs of sense to perceive unconsciously and for our minds to grasp.

The succession of elements of rhythm bounded by rows of horizontal lines guarantees us, indubitably and with a purely graphic clarity, the completely equal value of the rhythmic beats and confirms to us not just the identical character of the rhythmic feeling, but also the equality of the latter's harmonic qualities. Thus there is a strong increase in sensual effect in the rhythmic row in the second group of elements.

Another characteristic is that in addition to the main vertical rhythm, there is another kind of rhythm which may be traced. This is the diametrically opposite kind: the rhythm of horizontal articulations. Restraining and delimiting the harmonic essence of the main rhythm, this rhythm at the same time creates new repetitions and alternations which are full of their own special charm.

We have already examined this kind of phenomenon as exemplified by the rectangle, when studying the enclosed spatial form. In the latter case, just as here, there were two rhythmic streams flowing in opposite directions, but coming together in our minds to form a single unified rhythmic feeling.

And in just the same way, both in the formation of the architectural mass and in the particular articulations of this mass, we encounter the conflict of two opposite principles, a collision between two opposite rhythms. Here, just as there, the particular outcome of this conflict, the particular manifestation of this dramatic collision, is the exhaustive content of the work of architecture.

An extremely interesting manifestation of this inner life of architecture may be seen in any Doric temple in Greece. The cella stands on the stylobate steps fringing all four sides of the temple: this is the first group of elements of horizontal rhythm. Standing on the stylobate are the verticals of the columns, verticals which are reinforced by the fluting; these are the second and most important element of the collision. This is followed by further development of the plot. Again victory goes to the horizontal force in the powerful outlines of the architrave, but a little higher there is a temporary breakthrough made by vertical forces in the form of the triglyphs—in order to produce a final resolution through the resonant chord of the crowning cornice. Such in outline is the rhythmic content of the Doric temple.

In music we often encounter complex structures of this kind. You hear one voice—initially timid and unsure, but gradually growing until it is suddenly interrupted by another voice, which slowly condenses the rhythm of its sounds in order to discharge this dynamic collision with a unified lordly crowning chord. We see a conflict of two forces, two voices, two rhythmic streams—but as soon as we glance into the artist's creative laboratory, we realise that this conflict is simply a complex theatrical *mise en scène* where everything has been calculated in advance and where the author dilutes the rhythm of one stream in order to emphasise the strength and density of the other. And each little detail of the order, each curve of the *moulure* [decorative element] is a character in this spectacle; each accessory of the painting or sculptural decoration is an actor occupying the place which it has been shown by the director.

Likewise, both in the outline of the mass of the architectural monument and in the architectural articulations, both horizontal and vertical, within this mass, the true enigma of the essence of architectural monuments is in the conflict between the two rhythmic principles.

But in the Greek temple, as we have seen, all the wealth of articulations amounts to rhythms which are additional to or transmissive of the main and unified rhythm of the vertical columns.

Only in the inside of the temples (the Parthenon, the large temple in Paestum, the temple on the island of Aegina, and the main temple at Selinunte) do we find the use of two tiers to produce a solution—admittedly, as yet very timid—of the rhythmic task. The lines of the profile of the upper columns, continuing downwards, determine the dimensions of the first-tier columns. In other words, we may imagine a single column shaft encompassing two storeys and only accidentally divided by the architrave into two parts. Here the architect forcibly distributes the customary single-tiered rhythm over two tiers.

The passing of time, however, brought new problems. Roman architects were faced with more complex tasks in the rhythmic articulation of multistorey buildings. The need for amphitheatres with a greater capacity compelled the author of the Colosseum to articulate its mass over four tiers placed around a single central spot.

Here the architect applied the feeling of rhythm developed in him by previous centuries to a new problem; and this was the source of an utterly clear solution, the only solution possible given such an approach: to repeat the principal thought four times, expressing in this way the building's interior arrangement on the outside, clothing each tier in its own rhythmically manifested garment. We see four rows of the main vertical rhythms placed one above the other or, to be more accurate, one shared complex rhythm divided by architectural elements into four separate or, as they might be called, four *fractional rhythms*.

Their function in the present case is a matter of making the general subconscious feeling of rhythm tectonically coherent, explaining the essence of the architectural monument and preparing us to perceive the creator's overall concept, i.e. a matter of making the lyrical charm of the rhythm a rational and truly architectural instrument for use by the architect.

But in the present case the rhythmic task was nevertheless resolved fairly simply. And, in spite of the fact that the harmonic treatment of each of the fragmentary rhythms is full of the subtlest diversity of shades (in the lower tier the rhythmic module is a three-quarters column of the Tuscan-Doric order; in the second tier, a column of the Ionic order; in the third, a column of the Corinthian order; and finally, in the fourth tier, a flat pilaster of the same Corinthian order) the quality of the rhythm as such, i.e. the alternation of beats and intervals, remains identical for each tier, if we leave aside the fact that in the last tier the connective rhythm of the arch is absent.

However, the Romans have given us a rich supply of fragmentary rhythms. In the town gate at Autun (Porte d'Arroux), which is divided into two tiers, the overall rhythmic impression is considerably more complex. Between the two contiguous axes of the rhythmic modules of the first storey are situated three intervals (in the second storey). The quality of the rhythmic beats and intervals itself varies in the two storeys. At the bottom the beat consists of a monumental pylon; on top of the pylon is a slender fragile pilaster.

fig. 25

In the architecture of the Roman aqueduct in Nimes we likewise find a wealth of rhythmic content. The bridge is divided into in three tiers. The quality of the rhythmic beats and intervals is extremely simple and identical in all tiers (with the exception that the arches and pylons of the first tier are more massive than in the second), but between the contiguous axes of the rhythmic modules of the first two tiers there are four intervals instead of one in the third tier.

In both the last examples the dynamic pattern of the upper tiers is more intense; the coherent movement of the two fragmentary rhythms resembles the movement of two cogwheels, a large cog and a small one, which relate to one another in a ratio of 1:3 in the first example and 1:4 in the second. This is the same relation as between the bass and violin clefs—the cello and violin—in a musical orchestral arrangement.

The age of the Renaissance is characterised with respect to rhythm by an excessively developed element of alternation. The quality of the intervals and beats changes

fig. 26

at every other interval or beat, leading to the formation of two parallel rhythms which intertwine and chase each other, creating something like an architectural fugue. Bramante was a true master of this rhythmic alternation, which was given the name "rhythmic *travée*". In his articulation of different storeys, he created fragmentary rhythms of striking charm.

Of this kind is the treatment of the courtyard of Santa Maria della Pace in Rome, where the top storey has a rhythmic alternation of beats and the bottom storey has an ordinary repetition of these beats. Furthermore, between the axes of the rhythmic modules of the first storey, in the second storey there are two intervals instead of one. All this, as a result of the amazing harmonic treatment of the beats and intervals in both storeys, creates a fugue of exceptional depth.

But a particular complexity and richness characterise the fragmentary rhythms in the Cappella dei Pazzi in the Church of Santa Croce in Florence (designed by the great Brunelleschi between 1420 and 1461), this small but endlessly grand masterpiece of the Italian Renaissance.

fig. 27

While leaving the tempo of the rhythm itself, i.e. the order of the beats and intervals, the same in all three tiers, Brunelleschi resolves the problem of rhythm with the boldness of an innovator, the musicality of a composer, and the organic power of the architect of 'Divine Grace'. From storey to storey he stuns us with such a diversity and richness of form that we hardly know what to be more surprised at: the fullness and resonance of the fragmentary rhythms or the amazing wholeness and clarity of the overall unified feeling of rhythm. At the bottom the energetic beat is a succulent column of the Corinthian order, while in the second storey the beat is softer and breaks up into two small pilasters which barely project from the plane of the wall; and in the third, not at all tall storey the beat is strong, but short, materialised by the quadrahedral pilaster/pillar, which is shaped in full relief and surrounded by the dense shadow of the roof above it. At the bottom the rhythmical axis passes through the middle of a column; in the second storey, through the

fig. 28

spatial interval between two flat pilasters; and, finally, at the top, again through the middle of a full-relief pilaster.

What a powerful rhythmic instrument are architectural articulations in the hands of a true architect!

X.

We have thus sufficiently established that although the laws of rhythm are expressed in the formation of each individual architectural form, each particular arrangement of masses, *the true effective dynamic pattern of rhythm, however, is manifested most clearly of all in the regular alternation of rhythmic beats and intervals in the entire work of architecture, in the arrangement and shades of this regular filling of intervals.*

The quality of the beats and intervals is itself a secondary function of the rhythmic formation and constitutes a problem that is less important with respect to rhythm.

Thus in our desire to encounter the essence of the work of architecture—encounter its rhythm, abstracted from all other circumstantial qualities—face to face, and in our desire to highlight, among the multiplicity of characteristics of the work of architecture, its rhythmic qualities, we may easily arrive at a conventionalised stenographic transcription of works of architecture.

For instance, a simple rhythm, i.e. an alternation of particular highly simple spatial forms with rhythmic intervals (for instance, the prehistoric cromlech), may be set down in figure 29, drawing I.

Another example of the same simple rhythm is the naked architectural massif, where the stone material of the wall alternates with intervals of apertures.*

If the rhythmic module has horizontal extension, the same rhythmic problem may be depicted in drawing II.

In the event that the entire rhythmic action is developed in the opposite direction, i.e. when we look at elements of rhythm in a horizontal extent—the transcription will be similar to that in drawing III.

When the rhythmic module itself is made more complex, the overall pattern of the depiction will likewise be more complex. Drawing IV is a rhythmic beat consisting of two columns.

Drawing V is a transcription of a rhythm with beats consisting of one column in a large order and two in a smaller order, as in Palladio's basilica in Vicenza.

*) If the rhythm of the work of architecture is materialised only in the alternation of vacant apertures and wall material, then the rhythmic beats will be the precise borders of the apertures and the intervals will be the background of the walls against which the beats strike rhythmically. Naturally, the transcription will remain unaltered; only the content, concealed behind the signifiers of the rhythmic beats, will change accordingly.

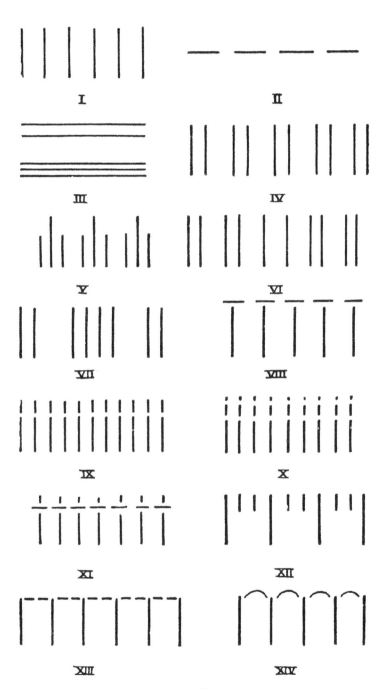

fig. 29

More complex rhythmic arrangements may also easily be set down using a diagram of this kind.

Drawing VI is the rhythmic arrangement of the Palazzo Vendramin-Calergi in Venice.

Additional rhythm, i.e. rhythm where the main rhythm of the principal beat is underlined by another additional

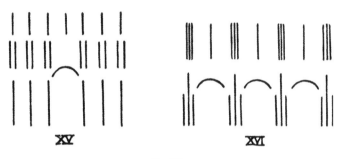

fig. 30

element of less importance, is represented graphically in drawings VIII, IX, X, and XI, where, depending on the character of the additional element itself, it is represented by a horizontal or vertical stroke. In drawing IX the additional rhythm is the vertical triglyph. In drawing VIII the additional rhythm is a horizontal mutule of some kind.

Drawing XI contains elements of additional rhythm in both horizontal and vertical directions.

Drawings XII and XIII are transcriptions of transmissive rhythm. In the first case the element of transmission is a vertical motif; in the second, a horizontal motif.

Drawing XIV depicts the connective rhythm of an arch or another element of whatever kind.

We may use the same method to set down more complex fragmentary rhythmic formations in a number of stages.

Thus drawing XV shows the rhythmic essence of the Cappella dei Pazzi in Florence, while drawing XVI depicts Bramante's rhythmic *travée* in the courtyard of Santa Maria della Pace in Rome (fig. 30).

In this way we may use this kind of transcription to depict the rhythmic content of any work of architecture, even the most complex.

The advantage of such a stenography of rhythms is that, leaving aside a certain conventionality, it contains an embryo of that sensual effect which is produced by the rhythm of the work of architecture. If we use scaled graph paper for these recordings, the same transcription will turn into a full architectural diagram of the building.

Rhythm will then acquire its static qualities on paper and we shall be dealing with rhythm which is architecturally materialised.

PART TWO

PROBLEMS
OF
RHYTHM

FOREWORD

Architectural style is an independent world, a distinctive and indestructible system of laws that explain and justify everything in that world. To understand style means to decipher these laws, to understand each element of form and the compositional methods which, with their help, create living architectural speech.

The architecture of China or India that enchants us with its strangeness is essentially alien to us not so much because its formal elements are unfamiliar to our eyes as because its compositional methods have yet to be deciphered and often seem to us incidental and unjustified.

However, what is incidental and unjustified is our approach to these works of architecture, for we have as yet been unable to *discover* these worlds, have been unable to identify the chain of laws which alone are capable of explaining everything—unable to fuse together the subconscious aesthetic pleasure of perceiving and artistic-scientific analysis of this art.

But if the so-called 'prehistoric' styles await their discoverers, then historical architecture too may to a certain extent be re-examined from this point of view.

The history of styles, as it has been understood until recently, is merely the history of the evolution of architectural form. The compositional methods binding these forms into finished buildings of artistic importance have remained in the background. However, here too identifying what is special about these compositional laws means completely understanding style.

For instance, Roman art, when viewed from the point of view of individual form, may be considered as nothing more than the Hellenist heritage in decline.

However, when seen from the point of view of compositional methods, this art strikes us with the wealth and diversity of its grammar.

Clearly, in conjunction with the history of architectural forms, a parallel history of compositional methods is also possible, analysing, above all, the moving force behind these methods, i.e. *rhythm* in all the diversity of its manifestations.

The present section is an attempt to identify and generalise these rhythmic methods. This means sacrificing the chronological and local frameworks that are usually employed in artistic-historical expositions.

I.

Each architectural form, considered in itself, is the result of rhythm: a particular quality and quantity of movement generates a particular character of shape. In just the same way that an entire group of architectural forms is, in the relations between these forms, a manifestation of related rhythmic laws.

Rhythm is the fundamental force, the complex of regularities, which governs the spatial distribution of formal elements and creates particular arrangements of these elements, gathering them together and compacting them in one spot and thinning them out in another, striving upwards and receding into the distance.

The overall outline of the Palazzo Strozzi, the mass of the Rucellai Palace, the order of the pilasters in the Cancelleria or of the window apertures in the Palazzo Pitti—all this may be explained by laws of rhythm.

But in just the same way as in an individual architectural form we identify the importance of rhythm in the formation of that form and see particular qualities in their static immobility (the harmonious state of form), so in an entire group of such forms the rhythm of this or that tension creates utterly distinct rhythmic formations which we treat as free-standing and independent problems.

We may distinguish a large number of quasi individual compositional methods with their own laws—laws which are often the opposite of the concept of movement of whatever kind, but nevertheless may also be seen as a function of the endlessly diverse laws of rhythm.

Thus the well-known *principle of harmony*, which distributes all elements in a static immobility where nothing can be made either larger or smaller, is merely a finished elaboration of particular beats and intervals in themselves and of a qualitative and quantitative relation between these beats and intervals, i.e. in other words, *a static development of the problem of rhythm.*

The *principle of picturesqueness* in architectural composition, with all the succulence of particular forms and the lack of constraint in the relations between them, is nothing other (as we shall see below) than a *rhythmic problem with sharply densified and unexpectedly thinned stresses.*

And even the principle of *monumentality*, which is diametrically the opposite of every notion of movement, seems to me, when analysed more carefully, to be an intriguing attempt to identify precise boundaries of rhythmic development—to, so to speak, establish a certain framework beyond which movement should not slip, i.e. *a striving to concentrate the rhythmic effect.*

Of course, any of these problems may be viewed from the point of view of precisely this distinctive quality. Thus, for instance, harmony may be seen from the point of view of the purity and perfection of particular elements of composition; picturesqueness, from the point of view of the richness and expressiveness of the moulures, forms, and silhouettes; and monumentality, from the point of view of its mighty indestructibility, tranquillity, and constraint.

Without going into a detailed analysis of the various compositional methods—given that these go beyond the bounds of the present investigation—I would like merely to show that in spite of this apparent contradiction, all this compositional distinctiveness is precisely distinctiveness of a rhythmic kind, that in a particular form, as in an aggregation of such forms, rhythm is the prime cause of particular formal consequences, and that individual features of the architectural style may be derived from this main law. But before moving on to consider these particular problems, I would like to identify this purely rhythmic principle *in its most unadorned dynamic state.*

I have in mind an ordered alternation of rhythmic beats and intervals, an alternation which is abstracted from other qualities of architecture; a movement of the elements which is subject to a clear and easily intelligible law, a law which is distinctive in its character of movement, but at the same time indeterminate in its boundaries.

The purely rhythmic effect is in itself fragmentary: no one requires that it have boundaries. The latter should not, however, be too short—if the law is to be comprehensible. When the law has been comprehended, further perception of its manifestations merely reinforces the pleasure.

It is indeed true that the beginning of any perception is always bound up with a certain activity of comprehension performed by the mind; the end of perception is bound up with a certain work performed in synthesising the impressions which have been received. And it is merely the intermediate part, between the beginning and the end, which contains the energy of passive, purely musical impact.

Of course, it is difficult to find a manifestation of the dynamic principle, which is so pure in its unadorned form. In materialising its laws in architectural forms, the architect always tackles his task using a particular compositional method whose functionality derives only from movement.

However, the architectural technique for creating enclosed courtyards decorated with a continuous row of pilasters, arches, or columns, makes this rhythmic principle sufficiently distinct.

It is indeed the case that in such courtyards we have a closed ring of rhythmic beats and intervals alternating with one another, without beginning and without end—a rhythmic strip of repetitions and alternations in which nothing halts the gaze or causes the consciousness to strive towards a singular particular spot. This technique was readily used by the architects of the Italian Renaissance in the inner *cortili* of palaces and monasteries.

In Bologna the same principle was transferred from the enclosed ring to a longitudinal composition, and almost the whole of this scarlet city is permeated with rows of porticos which pass continuously from one house to the next and from one street block to another—and even the out-of-town Church of S. Luca is joined to the city by a long thread of hundreds of individual arcades.

Even more than Bologna, Venice is characterised by a purely rhythmic sense. If we compare the life of other Italian republics, which are self-absorbed and live in the narrow field of their own interests—interests which may sometimes be great, but are always slightly provincial—with the broad, open, and showy life of Venice—with this fair of traffic between East and West, with this languid tempo of life, where there is no yesterday or tomorrow but a kind of fragmentary today which extends for ever—then we may understand why it is precisely here that this idea of utterly unadorned rhythm has been expressed so clearly.

In Venice, as soon as we place a foot on the bow of a gondola, we are already in the power of this feeling. The inaudible and gentle movement of the boat, the ever unforgettable rhythmic flexing of the gondolier, the unbroken fluidity of the canal waters, the endless lines of merging bridges and passageways: all this creates a magic of life which does not sit well with the precise flow of day and night.

In Venice it seems that everything has existed for ever and will exist for ever more and there is only Venice itself: a fragment of eternal duration, of constant

fig. 31

movement, of rhythm which is, above all, associated with our memories of this city.

The Palace of the Doges, the Palazzo Vendramin-Calergi, the enchanting lacework of the Ca' d'Oro, the Old and New Library, the Procuratie—all this is not so monumental, not so picturesque as before and, more than anything, it is rhythmic.

Indeed, the building of stone matter on the unsteady, untrue, mirror-like waters of the canals and lagoons is in itself non-monumental, as is the structure of the Palaces of the Doges, where we encounter a radical violation of the principles of monumentality in the very distribution of the volumes: at the bottom is a tracery play in stone, a delicate intertwining, while on top of this is a coarse heavy mass which threatens to crush and destroy everything underneath it.

The same may be said of almost any of the Venetian palaces; were it not for the necessity to create somewhere a spot containing the entrance, we would not find there a single centripetal idea—would not find a self-enclosed idea subordinate to the will of the architect.

But if we intend to look in Venice's palaces for a breakthrough into unconstrained freedom of the will, an incidental and succulent splotch of composition, a freely spread mass, or marks of picturesqueness of whatever kind, then we, of course, will be disappointed here too. In spite of the city's amazing atmosphere, its architecture is not in the least picturesque. On the contrary, this architecture is constrained by movement—not by the uneven and incidental movement of picturesqueness, but by the measured musical alternation of beats and intervals that provides the key to deciphering and understanding the architecture of Venice.

But, of course, most perfectly of all, this problem is resolved in the overall composition of Piazza San Marco with its ring of hundreds of arcades, where the understanding of beauty occurs in an unusual way. Here perhaps there is not even any need to look: the quadrangle of porticos has a hypnotic effect.

You can sit under the arcades for hours at a time without assimilating a single form, a single image, and nevertheless be enchanted by the rhythm of the overall composition. And we leave the Piazza not so much with brightly coloured memories as with scraps of the melody of a leitmotif.

Just as one should not dwell on a particular sound in a symphony, so we should not rip out from a ring a single link in the arcature. The four-cornered quad of the porticos of the Procuratie and the libraries and even the special luxuriousness of St. Mark's: all this is beautiful and valuable for the reason that they are rhythmic links in the same chain. And it remains a poignant mystery that the picturesque, rather self-sufficient architecture of St. Mark's, architecture which is alien to the entire ensemble of the square, nevertheless manages not to violate its rhythmic charm.

II.

The perfect creations of the sunset of the Italian Renaissance, whose richness and fullness of form and intensity and fitfulness of feeling are reminiscent of a mature and succulent fruit weighing heavily on the branches that have borne it, remained for a long time incomprehensible to both lovers of beauty and historians of the arts. The forms of the Renaissance seemed merely coarse; its abundance seemed importunate; its impulsiveness violated the cold beauty of Classicism. Only after the works of Gurlitt, Schmarsow, Wolflin* and others who discovered, you could say, the perfection of these works of architecture and defined the Baroque style as an independent phenomenon was it possible to construct a new compositional principle—the *principle of picturesqueness* with its own laws and consequences.

The age of the Baroque no longer seems to me an exclusive phenomenon of the decline of taste, and we have learnt to see the traits of this style even in ancient Roman art, which replaced the balanced and coldly beautiful forms of the Hellenes. The very notion of picturesqueness has become in our minds not an anomaly, but a rightful artistic phenomenon in which all the formal elements are just as regular as in the perfect works of Classical architecture and the Renaissance. This picturesqueness, as Veltlin did well to determine in his study, has nothing in common with vibrance.

The monuments of the ancient Classical architecture of Greece, which were almost always covered with bright colours, are absolutely non-picturesque. The way in

*) C. Gurlitt, *Geschichte des Barockstiles, des Rococo und des Klassicismus*, Stuttgart, 1887; A. Schmarsow, *Barock und Rokkoko*, Leipzig, 1897; Wolflin, *Renessans i Barokko* (Russian translation).

III.

IV.

which spots of colour are used and the alternation of these spots are essentially anti-picturesque. Indeed, let us look more closely at the reconstruction of an ancient Classical temple. What kind of impact on it does the bright colouring of parts of the temple have? The first thing that we cannot avoid noticing is that the colours underline the functions of all the details and deepen the character of the articulation, which is in itself by no means picturesque. Here the colour does not live, does not palpitate with its own life, does not have its own profound existence, but merely facilitates the revelation of other qualities which are distinct from the category of picturesqueness. Vividness is picturesque only when it is self-sufficient.

And, vice-versa, in a palace of the Baroque age it is easy to see how, without the involvement of colours and without any kind of colouring, a work can be created

fig. 32

which is palpitating, enchantingly unexpected, and animated by succulent spots of sunlight and shade—a truly picturesque work of architecture.

Clearly, what matters here is not that colours are involved in some way or other; colours are clearly not what is capable of making architecture picturesque. This picturesqueness, as a particular compositional method used by the architect, should, of course, be, above all, the consequence of the prime cause of any architectural form, i.e. of rhythm and its specific features. In what, then, are the specific features of the picturesque rhythm?

Let us look at two buildings on the Acropolis in Athens—the Parthenon and the Erechtheion, both of which are full of the element of movement. The Parthenon is elementarily rhythmic since the regularity of its movement and the composition of its concept are extremely clear. When we look at one of its facades, we are immediately filled with its rhythm, and our subsequent impressions are made easier by the regularity with which they are grasped. As we walk round all sides of the Parthenon, an ordered movement that has been given canonical form in the same way unceasingly penetrates our consciousness.

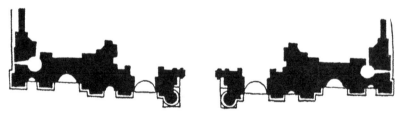

fig. 33

The essence of the dynamic pattern of the Erechtheion is altogether different. Here there is none of the constraint; the movement is freer and more intrinsically valuable. On the north side there is a single portico; on the east side, a portico of entirely different character; on the west side the portico has been replaced with a row of three-quarters columns beside the wall; and on the south side the portico has been replaced with a unique portico of "korai" or female figures (caryatids). All these elements differ from one another in every respect, including in their absolute dimensions, reliefs, rhythm, number and quality of beats, and the character and modenature of the Classical order.

Here we find a multiplicity of elements, a freedom of movement, an arbitrariness in the structuring of the masses, and a charming unexpectedness of overall composition. However, all this creative lack of constraint is seen, when analysed more closely, to be the result of more complex rhythmic laws.

The architect is by no means always satisfied with such a simple solution of the rhythmic problem as the simple repetition of beats in the Parthenon, just as the musician does not always confine himself to the elementary rhythm of the recitative. The primitive dances and songs of savages contain moments when the rhythm accelerates or slows down, a certain augmentation of dynamic effect following from an increase in intensity of perception. The law of movement becomes more complicated. The rhythmic beats and intervals are individualised, changing from wave to wave.

We have already seen a similar augmentation and diminution in symmetrical form: an axis passes through the middle of the building and on one side of the axis there is augmentation, while on the other there is diminution. Moreover, the laws of diminution and augmentation are absolutely identical. Such examples are extremely easy to find in Baroque churches in Rome.

In the Church of Il Gesù (designed by Vignoli) and Santa Susanna in Rome we can clearly trace this augmentation towards the central entrance and then a

V.

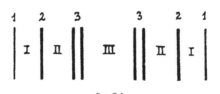

fig. 34

symmetrical diminution away from the entrance. In Il Gesù the effect begins with flat pilasters at the corner; the pilasters then give way to another pair of pilasters, which project in front of the first pilasters and then transition into succulent three-quarters columns framing the entrance. Here the quality of the rhythmic beats and intervals creates an intensification of effect with striking insistence (see fig. 33).

In Santa Susanna this rhythm is still more expressive since it is to be seen both in the elements of rhythm themselves and in the order in which they follow one another. The rhythm of this building is set down in fig. 34. Here the augmentation takes place in the spatial qualities of the beats (1: pilaster; 2: column; 3: double column) and intervals (I: almost smooth wall surface; II: niche with statue; III: unbroken aperture of the portal) and in the dynamic pattern of their movement.

The same law of rhythmic augmentation and diminution of masses is subject in the Erechtheion not to symmetry, but to optic balance. As we draw close to the Erechtheion along the main path, we instantly feel—in spite of the multiplicity of contrasting details—this optic equilibrium, which creates a particular symmetry in the general outline and in the silhouette of the patches of picturesqueness.

Still more typical in this respect is the propylaea of the Acropolis in Athens. Approaching the Acropolis,

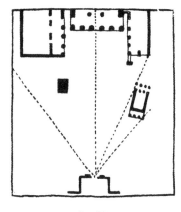

fig. 35

the viewer immediately felt the importance of this optical balance in which the lesser size of the right wing is compensated for by the fact that adjoined to it is the silhouette of the temple of the goddess Nike, making every detail in the composition individually distinctive. However, optical equilibrium likewise becomes a canon that excessively cramps the architect. The rhythm of augmentation of the overall pattern of the arrangement of the masses of picturesqueness breaks down into individual free-standing articulations which create freely diminishing or growing rhythmic beats. This results in the following: a wealth of articulations; the division of the whole into a large number of fractions and of each part in its turn into still smaller parts; a heaping up of details; thought broken up into an infinity of sounds; a strong stream fragmented into myriad drops. All the latter are symptoms of a restless and whimsical picturesque architecture.

If monumental art is always a creative synthesis of thought, picturesque architecture may very often be characterised as tense and restless analytical thinking by the architect. Through the fragmentariness of its articulations and the rhythm of the augmentation of each group of elements which create a whole series of seemingly incidental spots, this art strives for *indeterminacy, for indistinctiveness of overall impression*; the latter, after the distinctiveness of the canonical order of ordinary rhythm, seems to the architect to be a more worthy artistic means. In order to be sure of attainment of this goal, the architect resorts, in the end, to *destroying the precise contours and facets of the building*.

Endlessly fragmenting strict form, the architect is no longer content that the cube has turned into a polyhedron or that the number of facets is increasing without end; he takes this thought to its extreme and eagerly turns to the cylinder, the sphere, and to forms where there are no distinct orientation points and everything is dissipated in an endless rhythm of growth. But, after attaining this, he does not stop in his striving for picturesqueness: regular forms and circular volumes seem too primitively regular to him and consequently insufficiently picturesque.

And we may observe how in the art of the Baroque the regular circle gives way to the oval and the ellipse;

VI.

and the strict spots of the floor plans take on the most whimsical, monstrous, and indeterminate shapes. Where previously there was a right or acute angle and a determinate and hard facet, there now appears a soft, succulent curve, which smoothes out and blunts.

Even the hard plane of wall, which until now has been unshakably monumental, loses its tranquil clarity. An unswerving impulse bends this wall, forcing it to shiver with unprecedented life, giving it a crookedness that has never been seen before, and populating it with niches and dents, depressions and projections.

Finally, we see in the picturesque architecture of the Baroque age the emergence of impetuously dynamic elements such as broken cornices, nervous projecting consoles, and volutes with an abundance of inner life.

When we survey all this diversity of elements, it seems that anything and everything is now possible: there are no longer precise limits and laws governing the work of the architect. Living life has invaded the conventionalised canon, broken the unshakeable bases, and introduced passion and pathos and the insuperable boom of sea waves which grow and die down at the architect's caprice and whim.

A new weapon and powerful means in resolving creative problems, an instrument that is changeable and fluctuating, is the *play of light and shade, the way in which a work of architecture is illuminated.*

And indeed truly picturesque architecture shapes mass and detailing so as, above all, to produce light and shade, in the contrast of which all its restless essence is revealed. Before we are aware of lines and planes, we are amazed by the whimsical play of patches of succulent shade and bright sunshine. But not confining himself to the play of light and shade that he has called into life, the Baroque architect creates distinctively picturesque effects in interiors too.

An even and diffuse light, which gently and uniformly enwraps all objects, seems to the architect to be excessively primitive; he fills the space of the church nave with a gloomy twilight which smoothes over all the edges, making it impossible to find one's bearings in the volumes of surrounding space. The gold, the red velvet, the bronze, and the paintings of the chapels: all this merges to form a warm sensual atmosphere of indistinct and indeterminate spots. Moving forwards towards the central part of the building, we unexpectedly come to a halt, blinded by bright rays penetrating through the drum or basin of the dome. The architect's approach here is entirely based on this purely picturesque contrast.

fig. 36

In the choice and character of each detail and in the qualities of its modenature, we see a continuation of the effect of this new understanding of beauty. All the architect's attention is directed at choosing moulures, which are soft, succulent, and bulging and where shadows settle in dense and expressive blocks. There are no longer any dry or restrained forms. Everything that can generate sharp shadow, a living and free contour, and *a block of building rhythmic force* is called to life. We encounter details that are almost offensive; we encounter a mass of embellishments that threaten to flood the restraining forms. And if we look at the shaping of any detail in picturesque architecture, from the sharply curving line of banisters or the incredible positioning of a column in a special niche as if in hands which grip it tightly, to any cartouche or decorative figure—the focus of the architect's efforts everywhere indicates to us that *freely growing movement, passionate impulses, and contempt for clear and simple laws of rhythm are now art's mottoes.*

III.

In any architectural monument two opposite rhythmic streams are in conflict with one another—a horizontal rhythmic stream and a vertical one, whose simultaneous existence gives rise to a dramatic collision of architectural effect. And just as we have considered the rhythm of augmentation in one of these directions—the horizontal direction—just so we can trace the development of this problem in the vertical direction too.

This architect was sometimes led to confront this task by a more or less complex combination of fragmentary rhythms.

The bridge over the River Gard near Nîmes or the Porte d'Arroux in Autun are examples of a rhythmic effect which builds up from storey to storey. Multistorey buildings in ancient times were always of such a kind since the laws of structural statics necessitated making the lower storeys more massive and increasing their dynamism as the structure increased in height. Modern multistorey structures, which have overcome many laws of statics and are alien to the rhythmic laws of ancient times, on the contrary, embody the rhythm of diminution towards the top: at the bottom you have a sharply manifested dynamic pattern of narrow stabilising supports between extensive intervals of shops and offices, followed by a distinct slowing of the tempo in the upper residential storeys. But in both cases we see before us examples of vertical augmentation and diminution of the rhythm in articulations of the mass, the latter itself being inert and possessing little dynamism.

However, in the history of architecture there are examples in which this problem has animated not just particular articulations, but the mass of the building itself as well, imparting to monumental groups of masses of walls a life of movement and impulse.

The Egyptian pyramid shows the embryo of this dynamism in the diminution of the pyramid's facets towards the top. However, the general character of this rhythm is as yet insufficiently distinct. It becomes extremely clear in the *sacred structures of the Chaldeans, in ziggurat temples.* The observatory temple is devoted to seven heavenly luminaries—Saturn, Venus, Mars, Mercury, Jupiter, the Moon, and, finally, the Sun, to each of which there corresponds a particular tier of the temple, which is accordingly covered in a colour symbolising the given planet—white, black, purple, blue, red, silver, or gold.

But the rhythm of the Chaldeans is still very languid: the diminution towards the top is completed with cyclopic blocks of stone, rather than with individual articulated elements, and this upwards movement finds its expression in a certain augmentation of the rhythmic effect, an augmentation which is slow and drawn-out, with gentle ramps surrounding the ziggurat on all sides and gradually leading to the final, top, tier of the golden habitation of the sun. Here the monumental immobility is still very strong; the mass of the temple is inert, homogenous, and almost unarticulated; the rhythm of the growing effect encompasses this matter with incredible labour, trying to impart to it the possibility of speed, speed which slowly increases towards the top as it frees itself from the slab of stone.

And it is only many centuries later, in the age of the birth and preparation of new creative forces, when the mysticism of Medieval life again gave rise to an insistent and impetuous upwards striving, that we see another, more dynamic treatment of the same problem.

fig. 37

If the Chaldeans worked with an inert slab which unswervingly gravitates towards the ground and requires incredible strength if it is to be brought to life, the architects of the Gothic age, on the contrary, broke the entire mass up into individual molecules and atoms, and only then subjected them to the influence of rhythm. From this it is clear how obedient these elements were as instruments. The mass of the Chaldean monument is in itself opposed to movement of any kind, whereas the molecules of the endlessly articulated

Gothic churches are intrinsically dynamic, being small and directed upwards. The architect begins his work by placing narrow supports at the bottom; he then joins to them buttresses which increase in height and with

VII.

every step makes the rhythm still more complex until it passes into the arrow of a bell-tower pointing into space, an arrow which finishes with a minimum of matter—the blade of the crowning line of the cross.

And the exhaustive content of the Gothic cathedral is a development of the problem of rhythm of growing effect, of passionate freedom from matter and from the laws of gravity; it is a striving towards the enticing abyss of space.

Where is the connection between the naive architecture of the Chaldeans and the daring of Medieval man?

Instinctive resolution of the same rhythmic problem lays down a bridge between the centuries and reveals the eternal in the transient. And now, in an age when man stands on his own, far from both Chaldea and the Middle Ages—now this problem is again becoming close and comprehensible and the daring is just as enticing. All that is needed is new words, new forms which are distinct from the inert mass of the Chaldeans and the restless fragmentation of Gothic architecture—words and forms which you will never find anywhere apart from in modernity and which man will use to once again conquer space, as he already has done through the valour of his flying machines.

IV.

Studying the evolution of rhythmic tasks naturally brings us to the distinctive *problem of how to overcome rhythm*, a problem that resolves a dramatic collision of vertical and horizontal forces in a certain static calm.

It is necessary to create rhythm in order to be able to overcome it: such is the essence of the new problem.

The establishment of a limited number of rhythmic elements in the architectural monument is itself an expression of a conscious or intuitive striving to overcome rhythm.*

The kind of temple called "in antis", wherein columns were placed between the antis—projections in the longitudinal walls—(the Treasury of the Knidians at Delphi and the Treasury of the Sikyon at Olympia) pursued, of course, the same objective.

The architect of the Palazzo Vendramin-Calergi in Venice achieved the same by reinforcing the corners: by doubling the end columns, he created extremes of the rhythmic effect.

fig. 38

An utterly opposite, but nevertheless true method of overcoming rhythm is to create a strong central spot to draw attention to itself and thus halt the dynamic movement of the rhythm.

An extremely interesting technique for the mastery of rhythm, however, was created by the Greeks in the triangular line of the pediment gripping and enclosing the temple's columned rhythm.

If the rhythmic essence of any work of architecture is manifested in the struggle between the two dynamic principles, then a truly simple and brilliant resolution and

*) See chapter VII.

completion of this element of struggle is achieved by the victory of a new architectural direction, the sloping diagonal, a force which equals the conflicting principles.

The lines of the pediment resolve the overall tension of the rhythm and overcome its dynamic by creating a new reconciling direction, while their overall symmetrical arrangement in relation to the temple's main axis, the way in which they envelop and close off, creates a feeling of perfection and unity. These augmenting and diminishing lines convince us that the whole which is enveloped by them, for all the dynamism of the composition, is nevertheless subject to static laws too; that the action encompassing the temple is not unbounded, not incidental, but subject to the unified will of the architect, who knows when and how to stop it and where and in what way to set limits for it.

The charm of the Greek temple is so great because it contains not just the force of rhythmic expression, but also the truly brilliant might of the latter's being overcome.

It is extremely interesting to trace the essence of the Greek pediment through to the end. The pediment possesses a stunning depth of thought and an amazing consistency in the development of this thought. Finding a way out of the conflict between two rhythmic principles in the invention of a new—diagonal—principle, the architect exploits the enormous decorative space of the pediment and compels the sculptor to resolve the same rhythmic problem, regardless of the particular subject and content of the sculpture. Such are the pediments of the Temple of Zeus at Olympia. At its ends are two horizontals—recumbent figures. In the middle of one pediment are three and on the other, five vertically standing figures, pointing to the prevalence of vertical columned rhythm. Between them are a row of conflicting figures, which manifest in various parts of their movement a multiplicity of diagonal directions. Is not all this the exposition and development of the same rhythmic problem confronting the architect?

A still clearer manifestation of the problem is to be seen in Furtwängler's reconstruction of the western facade of the Temple of Aphaia on Aegina. In the centre is a single vertical figure, at the ends are horizontal figures, and between them is an entire series of group bouts in which there is a gradual augmentation of diagonal forces from the end horizontals to the central vertical. Furthermore, along

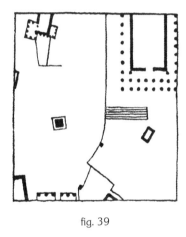

fig. 39

the axis of each column there is always a single horizontal figure whose proper regularity links both parallel rhythmic solutions (the sculptural and architectural) of one and the same problem.

In this way, in unfolding an almost continuous extent of rhythm in the longitudinal and secondary directions, the Greek temple creates a decisive overcoming of rhythm in the principal end facades. And when he looked at the temple from a certain viewing angle (the Greeks were very much aware that these are the most likely optical combinations), the viewer received the most striking impression. The main position from which to look at the Parthenon was undoubtedly, in the mind of its brilliant creator, from the northwest. From this viewing point the Parthenon comes across as most rich and monumental. And it is this point that has been used as the basis for the entire picturesque effect of the staircase carved out in front of the Parthenon.

In just the same way, the Temple of "Wingless Victory", the Temple of Athena Ergaiz, and the Temple of Artemis at Brauron are most impressive when seen from the side.

A measured succession of an unbroken row of columns, the completion and overcoming of rhythm using the same rhythmic means: this is wherein lies the unrivalled charm of monuments of Greek architecture. However, we shall also see the same principle, but in a slightly different treatment, in the art of later ages.

Cortili in palaces and *chiostri* in monasteries are examples of a similar continuous rhythmic stream of columns embellishing intimate courtyards; but when we step out of the courtyard onto the street, we always see the masses of the main facades, where, in addition to the overall rhythm, there is also the static force of the overcoming of this rhythm.

This problem is felt especially strongly in the layouts of complex architectural complexes, streets, and squares.

There is nothing more pleasant for the eye than a square surrounded by buildings with a continuous dynamic pattern of rhythm, among which the main viewing point is focused on a monument possessing the force to overcome this rhythm. That is why the memory of a quiet mountain village with a continuous rhythm of snowy peaks and the static vertical of a high bell-tower is so lasting. That is why we so value a wooden church with a bell-tower in the midst of the lines of the northern forest. That is why we find such amazing perfection in St. Mark's Square in Venice—where three of the walls framing this open hall are imbued with a tranquillising rhythm, while the fourth is taken up by St. Mark's Cathedral and the vertical of the bell-tower, which is the most beautiful and convincing example of perfection.

Since the most ancient times the overcoming of rhythm has led architects to an architectural problem in which static qualities oppose dynamic ones—to the problem of monumentality, a problem with which is usually associated the archaic stage of the development of each architectural style.

Of course, the architect's material itself, its inert qualities, and the slow tempo of the building process led, above all, to this primary task, and it was only as architectural mastery grew, together with acuteness of creative force, that more complex problems of rhythm came into being.

The very process of architectural creation is monumental: hundreds of hands leave behind traces of their activity on the monument. But often even a single work of architecture during the period of its creation outlives numerous human lives: one architect is replaced by another, then by another, and so on. 30 great architects, including Bramante, Michelangelo, and Bernini, followed one another against the monumental background of St. Peter's in Rome.

The cathedral in Milan was built during the course of several centuries; endless barges with snow-white slabs of marble moved slowly over the Italian lakes and then from there along the canals of Lombardy; there were chains of carts lumbering from Ferrara, Tuscany, Romany, and Piedmont; endless architects' commissions gathered on the roof, with a son often replacing his father when the latter died and where masters came together from all the ends of the world—Heinrich Parler from Gmünd, Ulrich von Ensingen from Ulm, Mignot from Paris, and also the great Leonardo, silently climbing the scaffolding of the incomplete building. The work of architecture was created over centuries and for centuries, while a person's life was an immeasurably small grain of sand compared with the life and dimensions of the monument.

Largeness of absolute dimensions was the first means available to monumental architecture. The large Temple of Amun at Karnak was 1,400 metres long and 600 metres wide; the Greek temple in Ephesus was 127 metres long; and the Church of Sts. Peter and Paul in Rome occupied an area of 3,306 square sazhens, having a length of 88 sazhens and a dome with a diameter of 137 feet.

However, an increase in absolute sizes is not sufficient in itself.

Anyone who has visited St. Peter's Square knows well the prolonged feeling which precedes the establishment in us of an impression of monumentality. We instinctively begin looking for a starting point for comparison in the cathedral itself. When we do not find it, we choose for this purpose a human figure that has incidentally caught our eye on the steps and, before we have come to the conclusion that the Cathedral of St. Peter's is indeed colossal, the thought occurs to us that man is infinitely small. At the same time, in monumental works the starting point for comparison usually lies in the building itself and is found at the first glance directed at the monument.

A conscious *violation of proportionality* is needed in order to reveal the monumentality through contrast.

Greek art of the fifth century, an age of brilliant flourishing (for it is only in an age of full flowering that proportionality, a thing of value in itself, becomes a desirable canon), has none of this feeling of largeness of scale. From the fifth century forwards, the Greeks shaped the order in compliance with the law of proportions, a law which is independent of scale. All the organs are subordinated to the modular canon; they are made larger or smaller in order to increase or diminish the module. When the length of the facade is doubled, the height of the doors and steps is also doubled—with the result that all connection between the function of these parts of the building and their dimensions is disrupted: the building loses its largeness of scale.

In a monumental facade, on the other hand, there should be detailing which is small, articulated—in order to underline the grandeur and unity of the whole. And it is best if this detailing is an easily comprehensible element such as the necessary size of the door, whose absolute dimensions are easy for the mind to grasp.

However, the problem of monumentality is still a rhythmic problem and, as such, usually has as its object rhythm in two directions. The distinctive rhythmic feature of this problem is that *development of horizontal articulations is to be preferred* at the expense of vertical rhythm. Let us compare the temple at Paestum with the Parthenon. How much more monumental does the temple at Paestum seem?

The Parthenon is abstractedly perfect in its proportions, in the reconciliation of the rhythms in both directions, whereas the temple at Paestum is aproportional and tends towards a prevalence of horizontal rhythms. The entire temple is lower, the columns are more massive, the architrave that tops the columns is thicker, and thus the illusion is created of intense work carried out by the load-bearing functions. The columns are thick, meaning that they can withstand a large load; the load is very large, so the gaps between the columns are also very large and the entire temple is very large, gigantic. This is the approximate path taken by our subconscious feelings when we look at the temple at Paestum, leading us to the synthetic thought that the Paestum temple is monumental.

Of just this same kind are the nature and significance of another technique, which consisted in *having the architectural mass and its elements expand towards the bottom*. Such are the entasis of columns of all kinds and the talus of the walls of Egyptian temples and other structures.

The problem of monumentality is also resolved by *tectonic treatment* of the walls of the architectural monument.

A wall divided into parts that correspond to its stone- or brickwork, or where the stone- or brickwork is exposed—produces an impression of monumentality, due to both the self-evident quality of the play of static and mechanical forces and the contrast between the small articulations of this element and the general surface of the wall. Thus in Greek architecture we always find these lines dividing the mass and its elements into individual stones and cutting through even the columns and decorative embellishments. Buildings in Lombardy and Romagna very frequently expose their brickwork, exploiting its aesthetic properties.

But it was only the Italian Quattrocento that took this technique to the highest level of perfection. In the Riccardi and Strozzi palaces in Florence the richness of architectural decoration is a matter of nothing more than rustication; the latter has the relief, weight, and massiveness of a load-bearing support. The arches of the semi-circular apertures are clad with stones which have been chiselled to form wedges and underline the solidity of the construction. The use of tectonics in the wall to increase the impression of monumentality reaches its brilliant apogee in the Palazzo Pitti in Florence. Here the rustication takes on a relief, might, and significance which is of intrinsic value in itself. The feeling of monumentality derives from each piece of rustication on its own and then increases boundlessly as a result of the overall impression made by the wall, which consists entirely of such rustication.

However, this kind of articulation of the wall is not centrifugal; it is subject to the unified will of the architect, a will which in monumental art encompasses every little detail of the monument, compelling these details to take part in resolving the overall problem, which is *to overcome the rhythm of the vertical articulations and allow room for free development of the rhythm of the horizontal forces.*

And if we turn to the most monumental art, the art of the Egyptians, where human life was understood only as an atom of cosmic invariability and not in philosophical abstraction, but in man's everyday outlook, we shall see this unity of thought and prevalence of horizontal forces and the overcoming of the latter at the top of the composition by means of a crowning convex element which casts a sharp horizontal shadow.

Greek architecture is more dramatic, but here too the collision is resolved by strongly projecting horizontal lines.

The age of the Italian Renaissance resolved this problem of horizontality to perfection, on each occasion underlining the tectonic divisions into storeys and confidently and powerfully subordinating them to the oppressive force of the crowning cornice (Palazzo Riccardi, Palazzo Strozzi, and other buildings).

VIII.

In the way in which the horizontal lines of the socle and mouldings follow one another—some, simple and severe; others, massive, elegantly slender, or with restrained decoration; some, projecting only slightly; others, casting a deep falling shadow—in all this we see the unrivalled mastery of the great age of the Renaissance.

And just as in the pure rhythm of horizontal extent there is a magic of purely musical feeling, so in the rhythm of augmentation and diminution there is a stirring feeling of picturesqueness, an overcoming of the principal rhythm; thus the problem of monumentality gives rise to a boundless sense of tranquillity.

V.

Rhythm is in movement. However, movement is in a succession of individual static moments. And the laws of this movement, like the laws of particular instants of immobility, closely intertwine with one another, in particular in the art of architecture, where of the two elements of movement—time and space—it is the latter which is the most obvious of all.

The dynamic pattern of the particular static moments of the architectural monument is a rhythmic manifestation of the monument. The charm of the static moment in rhythm is the harmony of the monument.

Clearly, harmony is that mathematical essence of rhythm which fills it with the material boundaries of matter and animates it with images of perfect form.

What difference is there between the eight-columned temple in Selinunte (sixth century BC) and the Parthenon (fourth century BC), these two so completely similar and at the same time different buildings?

The overall rhythmic content and character of the rhythmic beats and intervals; the style; the order; and the composition of the idea: all this is identical in both cases. However, these monuments may serve as the finest expressions of their ages—ages which differ in terms of outlook and means of artistic embodiment only because the absolute sizes of the beats and intervals are expressed by different numeric signs. The difference is merely in the different mathematical content of these two completely identical rhythms.

What is it, though, which serves as the unit of measure of this mathematical content—the *harmonic module* that, only in conjunction with the *rhythmic module,* exhaustively expounds the aesthetic significance of the work of architecture?

The Egyptians, who were the first to use brickwork for walls, inevitably and naturally arrived at such a unit of measure. All the bricks were made in a single size, and thus, since it was bricks that the Egyptians used as their principal construction material, all the sizes of the building were multiples of the dimensions of the brick. The brick was the first harmonic module, the first element used to structure the harmonic composition of a work of architecture.

Stonework made from sandstone of determinate dimensions likewise significantly simplified labour and thus it was that a new harmonic module was created. However, it was the Greeks who were distinctly aware of the imperfection and unreliability of this kind of unit of measure and tried to place it in an architectural element of some kind.

For the most part and almost without exception, regardless of the style and order of the building, it was the radius of the column which was taken as the harmonic module—as is confirmed by a number of documents from ancient times. Until the time of Pliny and Vitruvius it was thought that the module was the bottom radius of the column; however, checks conducted by numerous investigators indicated that this module is inapplicable to entire epochs during ancient times, including the Hellenistic period.

Sometime later, however, the French scholar Aurès managed to establish beyond all doubt that the module was not the bottom, but the middle radius of the column, i.e. *half of the sum* of the end radii. He proved that this module does not just relate to all the elements of the order in relations expressed in numbers very close to whole numbers, but also that this module is itself expressed as a very simple number in relation to the local unit of measure, specifically the Athenian foot.

Vitruvius points sometimes to the width of the triglyph and sometimes to the radius of the column as the module. Pliny asserts that the module was the radius at the base of the column.*

Establishing the existence of a harmonic module in a monument reveals the principal laws which defined the dependence between all the parts of the building and this module: *the law of whole numbers and simple relations.*

These laws of primary importance may be checked using the example of any ancient monument.

In the first volume of his *History of Architecture* Choisy adduces two very interesting examples confirming the undoubted importance of these laws. The first is an investigation into the temple at Paestum based on conclusions reached by Aurès, where with irrefutable clarity Choisy shows how fictive anomalies in this law may be eliminated. The second example is a surviving inscription from ancient times that contains conditions governing construction of the arsenal in Piraeus. The inscription makes it possible to restore this building. Both examples confirm both the law of simple relations and the law of whole numbers.

*) Auguste Choisy, *Histoire de L'Architecture.*

The numbers on which the latter is based—and likewise the correcting fractional number—are not arbitrary in Greek art. Often they derive from the enigmatic religious and scientific superstitions of the Greeks.* Thus, for instance, priority is given to numbers which are squares, based on the Pythagorean doctrines; next come odd numbers, which are regarded as "pleasing to the gods". Even numbers were systematically avoided. But the most favourable numbers were square numbers derived from odd numbers.

However, the harmonic essence of architecture is not exhausted by numeric laws alone. Very often, certain *graphic structures* are a canvas for the overall composition of a monument. As early as in the profound antiquity of the Egyptians, people knew of the right-angled triangle with commensurable sides expressed by the numbers 3, 4, and 5; this kind of triangle was given a sacral significance, as indicated in the tractate ascribed to Plutarch. The idea of the sacred triangle led Egyptian architects to think of establishing the overall proportions so that a triangle of simple outline could be inscribed into the building's plan.

Greek art is likewise subject to these geometric laws. Studies by Babin identify, in addition to the Egyptian triangle and its derivatives, structures based on the existence of the equilateral triangle and a triangle whose altitude is determined by its base being divided in accordance with the golden section.

---

*) Renaissance theoreticians were likewise not free of these superstitions. In them we see a strange intertwining of two opposite characteristics: on the one hand, a desire to identify laws of creation and a thirst for deliberate analysis of beauty, and on the other hand, all the constraint of human thought which looked for support in the superstitions of the ancient philosophers.

Vitruvius advises that in order to establish proportionality between length and width, use should be made of the relation of the side of a square to its diagonal. August Thiersch very cleverly proved, using examples taken from ancient monuments, a large number of more complex laws.*

But, of course, even more than in Greece during the heyday of Greek architecture, it is interesting to trace the development of harmonic art during the Italian Renaissance, and in particular during the Cinquecento.

Leon Battista Alberti, who stands between the monumental art of the architects of the Quattrocento and the harmonic ideal of the Cinquecento, was perfectly aware of this problem and clearly saw in it a large and diverse world whose laws he was keen to understand. More than his architectural monuments, Alberti's theoretical works bear witness to this. In his tractate *De re aedificatoria* he indicates that "a building should be executed in such a way that it should be impossible either to add to it or to change it without damaging the whole", i.e. he establishes the main principle of harmoniousness. But at the same time as Quattrocento architects instinctively tackled this task within the general scope of the inert monumental mass, Alberti understood it as consisting in the division of the whole into individual independent elements and in their harmonic coordination. In *Della pittura* he says that beauty has been spilt among individual objects and needs to be gathered together into a single whole.

The striving for *concinnitas*, i.e. harmonious proportionality of particular parts is a theme which passes through all his work.

*) *Manual on architecture*, published by Durm, IV, 1.

But what especially distinguishes the harmonic sense of the architects of the Italian Renaissance from the Hellenes is that the harmonic perfection of the latter was a canon which held them back from developing breadth and diversity in their creativity and made it possible, on the contrary, to deepen and endlessly perfect the smallest details. The *concinnitas* of Alberti, on the other hand, is much broader and freer; he does not try to establish a precise recipe for creativity and through his own works gives us an example of the multiplicity and flexibility of harmonic problems.

In the Palazzo Ruccelai he strives for harmonic perfection in the interplay between the horizontal and vertical articulations that dress the palace. In San Francesco in Rimini he sees harmonic perfection in the rhythmic principle of the ancient triumphal arch. In the portico of Sant'Andrea in Mantua we find certain strivings towards to the idea of "pure relations"'. And in Santa Maria Novella in Florence we see an extremely interesting composition where harmony had to consist in a balance of centrifugal and centripetal dynamic forces.*

But that for which Alberti strove and thirsted, it was *Bramante's* fate to realise. Bramante was a true master of harmonic art.

Although Alberti's works were, compared with the monuments of the Quattrocento, organisms which were

---

*) The top and bottom porticos of the church have articulations which tend to the golden section, but are opposite of one another: at the top the smaller element is at the ends; at the bottom the smaller element is in the middle. In the top tier the decorative motifs of the circles manifest a centripetal rhythm which is countered by the convergence of the pilasters at the ends. In the bottom tier the centripetal function is carried out by the rhythm of the niches and doors; this rhythm grows towards the centre; the centrifugal function is fulfilled by the use of a pilaster placed alongside the column to reinforce the corner.

articulated to a very large degree, it is only in the work of Bramante that we find an energetic overcoming of inert matter creating an organism which is *flexible and elastic, not so much clothed with articulations as consisting of individual members which exist freely but are nevertheless linked to one another.*

Architecture is a living organism like any other, and following this analogy we are accustomed to endow it with all the functions of organic life. In architecture we, to a certain extent, find the body and its members, each fulfilling their own function; often they are flexible, elastic, and consequently *harmoniously shaped.** The architecture of the Gothic age is shaped to an excessive extent. In the Gothic church there are 100 hands and 100 legs, so to speak; this is an organism which is nervous, exalted, dry, and impulsive, and in which restlessness and stress do not allow the members to develop harmoniously or cover themselves with the necessary musculature and flesh. The modelling is detailed, made from material that is hard and fragile.

The architecture of the Quattrocento, on the contrary, is insufficiently shaped. The organism of palaces by Brunelleschi, Michelangelo, Benedetto da Maiano is very simple, with few articulations; in most cases it consists of a parallelepiped and its harmonic essence is a matter only of a proportional dependence of the three dimensions and the arrangement of the horizontal rhythm of the cornices.

---

*) In *De re aedificatoria* Leon Battista Alberti says, quoting ancient theoreticians, that "a building is like a living creature". Luca Pacioli, a mathematician of the same time, indicates in his work *Divina proportio* that, "the ancients, when they got to know the regular way in which the human body is structured, built all their buildings, and especially temples, in accordance with its proportions".

And it was only the great genius Bramante who mastered the idea of harmonic perfection as no one either before or after him and truly employed spatial shaping in his architectural creations. He turned them into organisms with numerous members—members that are flexible, alive, self-sufficient, and at the same time harmoniously striving towards a single goal. He works like a sculptor chiselling his monument from soft and elastic material. The material of the Quattrocento is too inert; the material of Gothic architecture is too dynamic; but Bramante's material is precisely that consistency of mass which is required in order to surround certain volumes—i.e. for the plastic shaping of architectural forms in three dimensions of space.

And indeed Bramante began his architectural career in Milan with San Satiro, a building shaped like no other, and subsequently in Rome, as a mature artist, created the perfect Tempietto of San Pietro in Montorio and the brilliant design for the cathedral of San Pietro, buildings which enchant by means of their perfect modelling.

But, of course, Bramante does not confine himself to modelling parts of his organism. He also manifests an enormous ability to *link these organs to form a single whole*, to create a strong and indestructible arrangement for the mutual existence of particularities, to bind them together with an invisible but strong thread, and to reconcile the horizontal and vertical principles in a concordant existence.

The law of the triplicity of articulations, a law which has been well known from ancient times, is constantly employed in the work of Bramante too, in the horizontal distribution of the storeys and in the arrangement of the vertical pilasters (Palazzo della Cancelleria, Giraud). *The rule of the golden section* may likewise easily be checked using many works by Bramante. Wolflin in his study gives an extremely convincing analysis of the top storey of the side wing of the Cancellaria, where, moreover, the top smaller window is proportional to the large window and together they repeat the proportions of the interval which they have been allocated between the two pilasters.* The latter characteristic is of exceptional interest in the harmonic techniques used by Bramante and constitutes in his work the important principle of *repetition of particularities in the whole*, the latter principle being similar to a musical chord made up of concordant and related tones. Understanding the details provides a key to understanding the whole and, conversely, when the whole has been understood, the details are echoes, reverberations of the whole, vibrations of the air after the chord has already sounded.

All this endless wealth of harmonic techniques used by Bramante, a wealth which deserves to be studied on its own, creates—when there is perfection in the treatment of each detail and in choice of proportions which are light and elegant—an inexpressible feeling of *purification, liberation*, joy of being part of the world, joy which is full of satisfied perception.

The well-known and apparently unrealisable requirements addressed to the architect Alberti were fulfilled by Bramante to their full extent, thoroughly and completely, and even to excess.

VI.

What, then, are the results we have arrived at through consideration of these laws concerning various problems of rhythm?

*) H. Wolflin, *Renaissance and Baroque.*

Within the bounds of the development of each style, as over the course of the entire history of architecture, we may note a number of general—or rather, parallel lines in the development and succession of these problems.

In its architectural style, the *archaic epoch* in each culture tends to manifest itself through the grandness of the dimensions of the whole and the might and massiveness of the parts—which leads, above all, to the *problem of monumentality.* Such are the methods by which Egyptian architecture has its effect, and such is the archaic epoch of the Greek genius and the Quattrocento, the beginning of the Italian Renaissance.

Beyond this age in each style there occurs a period of brilliant perfection: *the golden age of art.* The immobile body of the architectural monument begins to come to life and the articulations acquire a certain energy of action. An elementary increase in the size of the module is followed by harmonic improvement of the interplay between all the elements. *The idea of monumentality* is sacrificed to the *problem of harmony.* This is the state of affairs in the fifth century BC, the century of Phidias, Iktinos, and Callicrates, the culmination of Greek creativity, and the sixteenth century AD, the age of Bramante and Raphael, the apogee of the new flourishing of Italian art. The perfection of the Parthenon and of the Cathedral of St. Peter is, of course, not in these buildings' absolute dimensions, but in the coordination of individual elements.

But art rarely remains at such a height for a more or less considerable period of time. Each peak is the beginning of a decline. Life increasingly takes possession of architecture. Rhythm becomes more intense, but also more anarchic in its nature. Articulations are dressed in clothing that is rich and lavish.

Just as the archaic age is characterised by the problem of monumentality and the epoch of the heyday of a style is characterised by harmony, so the *epoch of the decline of a style* has always been accompanied by the prevalent development of the *problem of picturesqueness*. The decline and disintegration of ancient artistic culture created the Roman style, while the destruction of the purity of forms of the Renaissance gave rise to Baroque, a style which is bent on resolving the problem of picturesqueness.

But the history of styles, like history of any kind, is objective. It knows no 'better' or 'worse' styles. A style exhausts itself to the very end. The problem is resolved exhaustively. A new input of creative energy, new geniuses, are required in order to once again begin the archaic age, once again proclaim the problem of monumentality. The continuous circle of stylistic development is closed.

However, the dead cannot be resurrected. It is always the case that the old problems are made more complicated; different methods arise for resolving them; and the creative elements which materialise the laws of rhythm—architecture's artistic images—change. As, of course, does the objective of modern architecture—which is to identify those elements of form and laws for combining these elements in which the rhythmic beat of our day will be manifested.

LIST OF CONTENTS

PART ONE

ANALYSIS OF RHYTHM

PART TWO

PROBLEMS OF RHYTHM

LIST OF ILLUSTRATIONS

DRAWINGS IN THE TEXT *

* The present illustrations to the text were not part of the plan for the present work. It was only the technical impossibility of obtaining the photographs I wanted at the present moment, coupled with difficulties of a purely typographical nature, that led me to this necessity.

The drawings have been put together—and some have simply been sketched—from engravings and are intended merely to illustrate particular qualities of the monuments.

Mospoligraf, 7th printing house

Filippovsky 11, Arbat, Moscow

Glavlit 5690   print run: 2,000

This publication is a facsimile reproduction of the Russian language original, published in 1922 by Mospoligraf in Moscow as an edition of 2,000.

Translation by John Nicolson.

Artifice books on architecture
10A Acton Street
London
WC1X 9NG
t. +44 (0)207 713 5097
f. +44 (0)207 713 8682
sales@artificebooksonline.com
www.artificebooksonline.com

Ginzburg Design Limited
12 Mulberry Place, Pinnell Road
London
SE9 6AJ
www.ginzburg-architects.com
info@ginzburg.ru

The book was published on the materials provided by Alexey and Natalia Ginzburg and Ginzburg Design Ltd.
Designed for the English language revised edition by Ana Teodoro at Artifice books on architecture.
Front and chapter pages revised by Ginzburg Architects.

All opinions expressed within this publication are those of the authors and not necessarily of the publisher.

British Library Cataloguing-in-Publication Data.

A CIP record for this book is available from the British Library.

ISBN 978 1 908967 86 2